Country & Western Dance

Country & Western Dance

Ralph G. Giordano

The American Dance Floor
Ralph G. Giordano, Series Editor

 GREENWOOD

AN IMPRINT OF ABC-CLIO, LLC
Santa Barbara, California • Denver, Colorado • Oxford, England

Library of Congress Cataloging-in-Publication Data

Giordano, Ralph G.
   Country & western dance / Ralph G. Giordano.
      p. cm. — (The American dance floor)
   Includes bibliographical references and index.
      ISBN 978–0–313–36554–6 (hard copy : alk. paper) — ISBN 978–0–313–36555–3
(ebook)
1. Country-dance—United States.   I. Title. II. Title: Country and western dance.
GV1623.G55   2010
793.3′1—dc22   2010012697

ISBN: 978–0–313–36554–6
EISBN: 978–0–313–36555–3

14 13 12 11 10   1 2 3 4 5

This book is also available on the World Wide Web as an eBook.
Visit www.abc-clio.com for details.

Greenwood
An Imprint of ABC-CLIO, LLC

ABC-CLIO, LLC
130 Cremona Drive, P.O. Box 1911
Santa Barbara, California 93116-1911

This book is printed on acid-free paper ∞

Manufactured in the United States of America

This book and my entire writing career
is sincerely dedicated to:
Debby Adams

Contents

Series Foreword

From the Lindy Hop to hip hop, dance has helped define American life and culture. In good times and bad, people have turned to dance to escape their troubles, get out, and have a good time. From high school proms to weddings and other occasions, dance creates some of our most memorable personal moments. It is also big business, with schools, competitions, and dance halls bringing in people and their dollars each year. And as America has changed, so, too, has dance. The story of dance is very much the story of America. Dance routines are featured in movies, television, and videos; dance styles and techniques reflect shifting values and attitudes toward relationships; and dance performers and their costumes reveal changing thoughts about race, class, gender, and other topics. Written for students and general readers, *The American Dance Floor* series covers the history of social dancing in America.

The multi-volume companion set in *The American Dance Floor* from Greenwood Press presents a series of shorter book length topics that focus on one specific genre of American social dancing including Ballroom, Country & Western, Disco, Folk and Square Dancing, Hip Hop and Underground, Latin, Rock 'n' Roll: 1950s, Rock 'n' Roll: 1960s, and Swing dancing. Each book follows a similar style and format so readers can easily cross-reference and compare the dances. However, each topic author has a specific interest and expertise in the specific genre. All of the authors have a thorough background in dance research, including scholarly research, years of participation, and for quite a few of the authors teaching the specific genre of dance.

Written in an engaging manner, each book tells the story of a particular dance form and places it in its historical, social, and cultural context. Thus each title helps the reader learn not only about a particular dance form, but also about social change. The volumes are fully documented, and each contains a bibliography of print and electronic resources for further reading.

Preface

I first learned to Two Step in November 1993. At the time, a friend who was working in Eagle Butte, South Dakota, had invited me for the Thanksgiving weekend and it turned out to be quite memorable. I remember landing in Rapid City with the temperature (not the wind chill) at twenty-three degrees below zero. Our Thanksgiving dinner of buffalo instead of the traditional turkey was surprisingly tasteful. But the next evening my friend took me to a place that I so fondly remember named "Boot Hill." It was a true honky-tonk that had a live country music band and a small dance floor. As the band played, she coaxed me onto the dance floor and taught me the Two Step. Some others also danced, while others drank, ate, or played pool. A fair number of the clientele were real cowboys right off the ranch.

Since that time, I became hooked on Country & Western dancing, and spent thousands of hours on the hardwood floor. At the beginning, it was often just my own little secret world. As I toiled away at my job during the day, I longed for the evening when I would scoot home and quickly change into my boots and jeans. I grabbed my cowboy hat as I left the house around 7:00 p.m. and headed into Manhattan for an evening at Denim & Diamonds. The franchise closed in about 1997 or 1998, but I still proudly wear my specialty denim jacket with the Denim & Diamonds franchise logo boldly embroidered across the back.

There was also a place that opened closer to home on Staten Island in an outer borough of New York. The place, named the "Pony Express," opened during the height of the line dance craze in the United States in 1993. It was located in the southernmost portion of

New York City; literally underneath the Outerbridge Crossing to New Jersey. It was absolutely huge, and on any given night it was packed with hundreds of line dancers.

During some stretches of time, I went seven days a week, usually to the Pony Express on Wednesday, Friday, and Saturday. At times, my son Jonathan also came to line dance on the club's Sunday afternoon family day. I also continued at Denim & Diamonds at least once a week and frequented other clubs close to home, such as the El Paso in Sayreville, New Jersey. I was so immersed that I also taught country line dance, as well as just about every type of Country & Western dancing. In that same sense, I was obviously heavily involved both in actually dancing and in learning a new dance style. I did not realize it at the time, but I was also absorbing the entire social atmosphere of the people, the music, the kinetic motion of dancing, and the "world" of country. Sadly, most of those venues I mentioned have closed, but we continued dancing and moved on. We spent over 10 years (and counting) once a week at the Whiskey Café in Lyndhurst, New Jersey. I would not trade those hours for anything.

As it turned out, the experience of participating in social dancing has provided me with a better understanding for completing this written historical work. Since I started Country & Western dancing my wife and I have danced in twenty-three states in America, and six other countries, visiting hundreds of dance clubs—probably a thousand or more if we include outdoor dance events, dance studios, and dance weekends. Dance historian Lloyd Shaw probably said it best when he wrote: "It isn't enough to read such books, you get only part of their impact. But if you put on a phonograph record, and dance, you get a moving, kinetic, living idea of what it's all about" (34).

We have never applied our dancing for competition because that would take the fun out of it. In all instances, that is simply not why people go out dancing. Through all the years and places that I have danced, I have observed that people do it because it is fun, it is sociable, and it is a time to forget the realities of the world's abuses. All too often, dance competitions, especially those on television, try to place competition upon dancing with an abstract known as "winning" being the only goal. This approach subtly forces many to sit by idly and observe rather than participate. In reality, that is certainly not what dancing is about; nor, for that matter, do people really understand what "winning" is about. For us, during one stretch of about 18 months from 2005 to 2006, we saw a friend bravely battle cancer. Despite it all, each week she line danced at one of our regular country dance venues, The Whiskey Café. Sometimes the chemo treatments limited her to only a few minutes and she had to go home early, but she persevered and got stronger and healthier. She has certainly appeared to beat the odds and is once again line dancing many hours a week—that is winning!

Acknowledgments

As we begin this series on *The American Dance Floor*, I am elated about this project on Country & Western dancing. The opportunity would not have happened without a contract not only for this book, but also for the entire series from Greenwood Publishing. The idea started when Greenwood's Debby Adams contacted me about the idea. (We had worked together on three previous books.) During the developmental stages of selecting titles and authors, Debby left Greenwood and was replaced by George Butler. The transition was seamless and George has proven quite helpful.

Researching a book is not accomplished without the assistance of some very talented and dedicated people. Research for all of my books to date has been ably provided by Angie DeMartinis. Her promptness and professionalism in servicing my interlibrary loan requests was invaluable. Thanks go to contributing sources for photographs to those that include the Associated Press, Graham Beech, Bettmann/ Corbis, Steve Clarkson, Dancin' Cowboy, the Frank Driggs Collection, Getty Images, Matthew Giordano, Hunter Textbooks, Library of Congress, the Michael Ochs Archives, Mike's Music and Dance Barn, Photofest, Sigma Press, Thelma Lynn Olsen, Frank Rogoyski, Steve Dean and the Texas Dance Hall Preservation, Inc., the University of Texas Press, the Wildhorse Saloon, James M. White, Richard Galbraith, Aaron Latham, Paul Bartz of Windwood Theatricals, Judith Temple of Kendalia Halle, and Paul Efird, Director of Photography with the *Knoxville News Sentinel*. A special thank you to Jane Thacker for taking me to "Boot Hill" in South Dakota for my first Two Step. I have been most fortunate to have worked with such wonderful individuals and companies. Throughout it all, I have always had the support of my family, especially my wife, Thelma Lynn Olsen, and our children, Matthew, Jonathan, and Laura. For all of that, please accept my gratitude.

Introduction

Country & Western dancing is a genre that has been hard to define. Basically, the term "country dancing" was loosely applied to any dancing done in the countryside or just about any rural area. In that sense, just about any type of Appalachian Mountain Dancing, English country dancing, square dancing, barn dancing, and other similar events were often called "country dances." One example was the Playford style of English-country and contra dancing that traced its roots to 16th century England and France. The styles were copied and danced in the American colonies and sometimes called American country dances. By the mid-1800s, that type of country dancing was passed down among generations in the American Appalachian mountain regions, but was far removed from urban dance styles and from the region of southwestern America. In other areas, the country dances in the English Playford and American colonial styles were displaced from the social dance scene in favor of Quadrilles, Lancers, the Waltz, and the Polka, among others. All of those also got mixed up in a myriad of folk, square, circle, and round dances in many regions of America. Although most of the same dances found their way across the country, simply put, if a style was not danced in an urban ballroom with strict etiquette rules, it was lumped together with other styles and classified as "country dancing." By the late 1800s, with the American westward migration across the continent in full swing, this type of dancing was also sometimes called "western dancing."

By the 1890s, and especially during the 20th century, it is suffice to say that the trend in American social dancing and music was divided between urban and rural areas. The urban areas were heavily influenced by the ethnic contributions of African Americans and newly arriving immigrants of Jews, Italians, and, later, Latinos. Many new dances such as ragtime Animal dances, the Charleston, the Lindy Hop, and others originated among less wealthy immigrants and ethnic populations. In time, however, these styles were danced in a myriad of urban dance halls ranging from the totally downtrodden to the extremely elegant and grand.

The roots of Country & Western music and dancing are linked with the folk music that English, Irish, and Scottish settlers brought to the Appalachian Mountain region of the South in the 18th and 19th centuries. English ballads and Irish reels, in particular, also had a major early influence. Such music was performed in colonial times in both religious and social contexts, including church services, weddings, and barn dances. Those same roots contributed to Square Dancing that was most often associated with, and at the same time, most often confused with Country & Western dancing. However, square dancing developed its own unique style incorporating elements of the Waltz, Polka, Schottische, and mainly the Quadrille, but was substantially different than Country & Western dancing.

An often overlooked historical fact is that Czech immigrants contributed immensely to the rich country western dance history not only of Texas, but also of America. Michael Corcoran, in a research article for *Austin360.com*, noted that the Czech influence began as early as 1852, when Galveston Island was settled by 16 Czech families who were followed by another 15,000 or so up until 1900. The Czechs brought with them traditional folk music and the polka dance. (The Polka originated around 1822 in the Bohemian region of the Czech Republic and Slovakia. It was introduced to America in 1844.) Recognizing the need for entertainment, the Czech settlers built community halls in Texas, mainly for dancing, such as Fischer Hall, 20 miles west of San Marcos, and Sefcik Hall, eight miles east of Temple. Sefcik Hall, as one example was a later addition, built in 1923 and named after its owner, Tom Sefcik. In a 2007 interview with Corcoran, manager Alice Sulak—who at 74 years old had managed Sefcik Hall almost her entire life—noted that very little had changed since the hall first opened. She did note the addition of a wooden dance floor in 1953.

She said, "We have all kinds of people coming to Sefcik Hall. . . . But the one thing they all have in common is that they love to dance."

At the same time that Czechs were settling in the region during the 19th century, a significant number of German immigrants also settled in Texas areas such as Fredricksberg and New Braunfels. They also brought European traditions of music and dancing. In that same tradition they also built community dance halls. In Comal County, which is located within the city of Austin, one example was Saengerrunde Halle. Corcoran noted that Saengerrunde Halle, as did so many others, served many functions. He wrote, "These halls were meeting places where such topics as life insurance and livestock protection were discussed during the week. And on Saturday night, the community danced." In similar fashion, southwestern music and dancing was influenced by other ethnic groups, such as Spanish and Mexican descendants who traced their roots to 16th century settlements in America. For the most part, however, these groups were often segregated from whites. By the turn of century, the early 1900s introduced a fusion of many musical styles evolving into uniquely new styles of American music and dancing. In similar fashion, each new trend in music was a cause that triggered the effect for a new dance style. Ragtime music spawned animal dances; jazz the Charleston; swing the Lindy Hop; Latin music the Mambo and Cha Cha, and the many Rock 'n' Roll dances such as the Twist, among many others. And, of course, Country & Western the Two Step.

The definition of Country & Western dancing in the sense that it came to be known from the 1920s and into the 21st century can be traced to when the dancing and the music went together. The beginning, therefore, can be applied appropriately to the development of Western Swing music in the rural southwest areas of Texas and Oklahoma during the 1920s. At about the same time, American music was generating the birth of the totally new American art form of jazz music. This new syncopated jazz music was accompanied by new dancing styles, including the Quickstep, Black Bottom, and the unforgettable Charleston.

The early western swing bands were heavily influenced by the syncopated sounds and improvisation of jazz, and often played jazz and ragtime tunes. The regional bands that toured the geographical southwestern panhandle areas of Texas and Oklahoma eventually expanded their range, mainly due to radio and, later, Hollywood movies. The music itself changed in terminology, mainly categorized by trade magazines such as *Billboard* and *Variety*. At first they called it Hillbilly, followed by Folk, Country & Western, and by the late 20th century, it was simply known as "Country" music. Throughout that time, some sub-genres included Western Swing, Honky Tonk, Outlaw, Rockabilly, Bluegrass, the Nashville Sound, and New Country, among others. Regardless of the style, people danced to the music.

1

Western Swing
and Crystal Springs

"We was just tryin' to find enough tunes to keep 'em dancin."
—Bob Wills

The beginning of "Country Music" dates to August 1, 1927. On that day Jimmie Rodgers and the Carter Family recorded for Victor Records in Bristol, Tennessee. The Carter Family recorded old traditional Appalachian style fiddle tunes. Rodgers, on the other hand, was noted for a "unique" singing style and recorded sentimental ballads, including "The Soldier's Sweetheart" and "Sleep, Baby, Sleep." James Charles "Jimmie" Rodgers (1897–1933), born in Meridian, Mississippi, was often called the "Father of Country Music." In a career sadly shortened by ill-health, he never appeared on any major radio programs, nor did he appear on the celebrated Grand Ole Opry. Nevertheless his prominence was so revered that, in 1961, he joined Fred Rose and Hank Williams as the first inductees into the Country Music Hall of Fame. Although the styling of Jimmie Rodgers and the Carter Family was classified as the beginning of "country music," it was not always music performed specifically for dancing (Roughstock's, "The Beginnings").

Some say that the first commercial recordings of "true" country music were done in 1922 by Eck Robertson and Henry C. Gillilant for Victor Records. The first "singing cowboy" might well have been Vernon Dalhart of East Texas. In 1924 he made some recordings in New York City that proved popular. His double-sided "The Wreck of

1

the Old 97" and "The Prisoner's Song" sold over one million copies and made him what was most likely the first country music star. Robertson, Gillilant, and Dalhart opened the door for the likes of Carl T. Sprague, Ken Maynard, Tex Ritter, Gene Autry, and Jimmie Rodgers to record country music. Maynard might actually have been the first Hollywood "singing cowboy," appearing in the 1930 film *Song of the Saddle* (Treviño 2002, 1–2; Casey 1985, 42).

During the late 1920s and throughout the 1930s, country music was described by many different names, including "Fiddle," "Hillbilly," "Western," "Folk," "Country," "Texas Swing," and "Country & Western," among others. Record and radio executives, on the other hand, simply classified it all as "Hillbilly." Whatever the classification, the southern style of music was mainly regional. The first broadcast of the regional style was from the Atlanta radio station WSB in 1922. As for radio "dance shows," WBAP in Dallas broadcast a weekly barn dance show specifically for square dance. In 1924, WLS in Chicago created a national network broadcast of country-style music on the show, "National Barn Dance." By 1927, WSM in Tennessee had launched the "Nashville Barn Dance," a regional musical stage and radio show playing Country & Western records featuring the Carter Family and Jimmie Rodgers. WSM later changed the name of the show to the famous "Grand Ole Opry," which was broadcast over much of the nation (Boyd 1998, 9).

Although it might not have had an official designation, the country music of Western Swing developed from a combination of Jazz, Dixieland, Blues, and Fiddle, among other contemporary American rhythms. In fact, at the time that jazz was sweeping the urban areas, music historian Jean A. Boyd in *The Jazz of the Southwest* simply noted "Western Swing was jazz created by and for country folk" (1). In similar fashion, Roughstock's History of Country Music described Western Swing as "Saturday night dance type of music, which combined the style of jazz and big band swing with the culture of the Southwest" (Roughstock's, "Western Swing").

As the depression swept across America during the 1930s, so did swing music of the Big Bands. Most Americans listened to swing on the radio. By 1930, radio was an inexpensive form of entertainment and many southwestern musicians were afforded the opportunity to hear the same radio music as the rest of the nation. In turn, the musicians of the Southwest combined their Country & Western music with the influences of contemporary urban big bands. Thereafter, western swing solidified as a truly distinct American music form. However, as music historian Murray L. Pfeffer explained, "It differed from the big bands in that the instrumentation was not the same, and the style was more ensemble playing for the simpler 1 and 2 step dances." Similar to the big bands, the "simpler" Country & Western dances included the Fox Trot, but unlike the big bands, western swing also played Mexican influenced waltzes and ethnic influenced polkas. Unlike the dominant multi-brass and horn instrumentation of the big bands, the bands of the southwest most often featured fiddles and guitars. Whether the genre was named or unnamed, Western Swing during the 1920s and 1930s was certainly defined by the accompaniment of a new style of dancing that was distinctly Country & Western. The main focus of the music was to keep people dancing, and two of the early proponents of western swing as dance music were Bob Wills and Milton Brown (Roughstock's, "Western Bands History").

A "dance orchestra" in McIntosh, Oklahoma. Oftentimes, a fiddle and a guitar were the only components needed for dancing. Many of the early western swing bands such as Bob Wills and Milton Brown began their careers in similar fashion. (Library of Congress, Prints and Photographs Division LC-USF351-312.)

Bob Wills, the "King of Western Swing"

Bob Wills was often called the "King of Western Swing" and Milton Brown the "Father of Western Swing." In later generations, Wills was better known and left a lasting impression, influencing many other Country & Western musical artists. That larger influence, however, resulted mainly because Milton Brown suffered an untimely death during the mid-1930s. In fact, the term "western swing" was not officially adopted for the music genre until well after World War II, when it was applied to Spade Cooley. Although the titles were bestowed on both Wills and Brown many years later, both men were founders of the new genre of Country & Western dance music that began during the 1920s.

James Robert "Bob" Wills (1905–1975) was born and raised in West Texas, an area comprised mostly of ranches and open range. At the time, the prominent traditional choice of entertainment was dancing to fiddle music. Both Wills's father and grandfather played music at ranch dances as "breakdown fiddlers" accustomed to playing for folk and square dancing. In turn, Bob also learned the fiddle at a young age and played fiddle music at a ranch dance as early as 1915. As the story goes, Wills's father John could not be at a particular dance. In his place, the 10-year-old Bob played alongside his grandfather. Although the young Bob only knew a limited number of dance tunes, apparently the dancing went on without nary a complaint (Townsend, "Homecoming").

In subsequent years, Wills performed at other ranch dances in West Texas. He played the same breakdown fiddle and folk tunes as his father and grandfather. The distinct style of the breakdown folk tunes maintained a consistent "two-four dance beat." It was that same dance beat he had learned from his family that Wills would maintain in all his songs throughout his long career. After World War I, Bob Wills left home and sought to earn a living playing dance music. But before he left home, he was also strongly influenced by a local band known as the Stockletts. Of the Stockletts, Wills said they had "the best fiddle band for dancing" that he had ever heard (Townsend, 38–39).

During the 1920s, business was prosperous in the cities, but farm life was hard. Before the Depression actually began with the stock market crash in 1929, a severe economic downturn was evident among rural farms and ranches as early as the mid-1920s. Although they were musicians, the Wills family was not immune to the economic crisis. During the 1920s, and especially later during the Depression, simply playing fiddle music at a dance did not pay a lot of money. Therefore, many musicians kept working at farm and ranch life as well as playing music. According to biographer Charles R. Townsend, the Wills family "worked in the fields all day and played dances at night to earn a living and make mortgage payments on their river farm." As a result, many down-on-their-luck individuals sought expression in music. One such form, especially among African Americans, was the Blues. Unlike the fast-paced syncopated style of contemporary ragtime and jazz, the Blues emoted the reality of hard times, segregation, and economic misfortunes. Through his touring later on, Wills was exposed to blues singing and listened closely. He was particularly enamored of Bessie Smith's style. Soon thereafter, Wills incorporated the influences not only of blues, but also jazz with his fiddle-style dance music. Some of the syncopated jazz rhythms were applied to the faster triple-step Polka dancing, while the Bessie Smith styled blues songs were applied to the slower dances. Among African Americans, the slow dance was known as the "slow drag," but among the Country & Western set it was known as the "buckle polisher" (Townsend, "Homecoming").

The Light Crust Doughboys

By 1929, as the depression hit nationwide and farms failed rapidly, Wills moved to Fort Worth, Texas, seeking full-time work as a musician and entertainer. In a short time he met guitarist Herman Arnspiger and formed the Wills Fiddle Band. They played some shows and dances in the Fort Worth area. At one dance, Wills encouraged a guest vocalist named Milton Brown to join them onstage. Wills was impressed and asked both Milton and his brother Derwood to join the Wills Fiddle Band.

Milton Brown (1903–1936) was also born in Texas in Stephensville. His family had relocated to Fort Worth in 1918, and throughout the 1920s he worked at various jobs and at one time as a salesman. At the onset of the Depression, he, along with millions of other Americans, lost his job. Shortly thereafter, in 1930, he was at the dance in Fort Worth and joined the Wills Fiddle Band. By that time, Wills, Arnspiger, and brothers Derwood and Milton Brown were offered a regular radio spot on WBAP (Erlewine, "Milton Brown").

The WBAP radio program was sponsored by the Aladdin Lamp Company, which in turn had the band change its name to the Aladdin Laddies. At the time, radio was a profitable venture and by 1930 almost all American homes had access. It was common at the time for businesses either to name a musical band—or even the entire radio program, after a commercial product. The following year, the band signed a commercial radio deal with Burrus Mill on KFJZ and once again changed their name, this time to the Light Crust Doughboys.

The name change for Wills and the other band members came solely as the result of monetary sponsorship by W. Lee "Pappy" O'Daniel (1890–1969), who was the president and general manager of Burrus Mill. (O'Daniel was later governor of Texas and also a U.S. senator.) The main product of O'Daniel's Burrus Mill was Light Crust flour for baking goods. In turn, he ventured onto the commercial radio airwaves to promote and sell his product. For the Light Crust Doughboys, the exposure offered by the sponsorship of the radio program made the band well-known across the region. At first, the Forth Worth radio show went on at 12:30 in the afternoon. A few months later it was expanded and picked up over WOAI in San Antonio and KPRC in Houston. Within the year, the show was broadcast over 170 radio stations by the Southwest Quality Network, and could be heard all through the Southwest. As a string band, their radio popularity was linked to playing music appropriate for dancing. The main ingredient according to Derwood Brown was, "We listened to all kinds of music, but especially whatever kind of music people danced by." In early 1932, as the Fort Worth Doughboys, the band also recorded a few of their dance tunes for Victor Records, including "Sunbonnet Sue" and "Nancy Jane" (Townsend, "Homecoming").

The music played on the radio and recorded on Victor Records by The Light Crust Doughboys was purely dance music. Therefore, it was only logical that playing that same music at local dance halls would have meant additional money for the band members. However, O'Daniel did not want the band playing anywhere other than at the radio promotion for his flour company; nor did he want to pay them any more money. As a result of these differences, in September of 1932, Milton and Derwood Brown left The Light Crust Doughboys and formed their own band.

Milton Brown the "Father of Western Swing"

Without missing a beat, they named their new band "Milton Brown and His Musical Brownies," which some music historians claim was the first Western Swing band. Biographer Cary Ginell, for example, credited Brown as the founder of western swing, and music historian Robert Palmer added that the Musical Brownies "virtually invented the wonderful hybrid known as western swing" (Ginell 1994, xxi; Erlewine, "Milton Brown"). The Musical Brownies also secured a deal with rival local radio station KTAT. In a short time, they were a favorite in the Fort Worth area and attracted large crowds at the local dances. Their musical style was a similar blend to Wills's that included a mix and influences from contemporary pop tunes, jazz, the big bands, and Country & Western. Music historian Murray L. Pfeffer said that the Musical Brownies "had a harder dance edge than their predecessors." Mainly, it was the unique vocal styling of Milton Brown that gave the band its unique flavor (Pfeffer, "Western Swing Bands History").

Unlike many other southwestern dance band members, Milton Brown was solely a vocalist and did not play any instrument. Brown's musical tastes were varied and usually included updated versions of old classics or contemporary standards. One music historian noted, "Brown could, and did, sing just about everything, from straight pop to sentimental old ballads, heartfelt blues to jazzy hipster jive, cowboy song to country hoe-down." His songs included, "Darktown Strutter's Ball," "St. Louis Blues," "Texas Hambone Blues," "Easy Ridin' Papa," "Joe Turner's Blues," "The Sweetheart of Sigma Chi," and "Garbage Man Blues," among many others. Of particular note was Brown's musical adaptation of two turn of the century blues ballads, "Corrine Corrine" and "Sitting On Top of the World." Musical artists of all genres also recorded each of these songs countless times throughout the 20th century. With the Musical Brownies they were slightly re-titled "Where You Been So Long Corrine" and "Just Sitting On Top of the World" (Erlewine, "Milton Brown").

Milton Brown and His Musical Brownies were immensely popular, especially throughout Texas and Oklahoma. The contributing factor was the daily radio program on KTAT and later in 1935, on WBAP—a 50,000 watt radio station in Fort Worth that covered the entire state of Texas and significant portions of Oklahoma, Louisiana, and Arkansas.

The radio exposure not only increased the band's popularity, but also its demand at dances. The Brownies eventually bought a touring bus, performing in remote dance halls, such as in Crowell, Texas, a town located about 200 miles northwest of Fort Worth with a population of about 2,000. Despite the small population, dance halls such as those in tiny Crowell often packed in 200 to 400 dancers. As was typical for many bands at the time that both toured and had regular radio programs, the grueling schedule meant that the band members usually had to return home each morning to Fort Worth, not only for the daily radio program, but also to play at Crystal Springs Dance Hall (Ginell, 141–142).

Crystal Springs Dance Hall

Almost universally, all music historians agreed that Brown's Western Swing began at the Crystal Springs Dancing Pavilion in Fort Worth, Texas. Crystal Springs, located at 5336 White Settlement Road, was a semi-legendary address for the Depression-era folks in and around Fort Worth. It was named for the private pavilion and small recreation facility that was built shortly after World War I by Samuel "Papa Sam" Cunningham around a lake that possessed natural spring water. It was later converted to a public dance hall and "officially" opened to the public on March 25, 1925, advertising both "Dancing and Swimming." Admission to the pavilion was priced at 40 cents for men and 10 cents for women. The pavilion was located on a sloping downward site towards the lake and a swimming pool. Those who wished to dance entered the hall at grade level from the parking lot on the high side of the slope. Down the slope and around the back of the building and underneath the dance floor was a changing room for those wishing to swim in the lake or pool (Ginell, 115–116, 135).

During the late 1920s, Crystal Springs was not overly popular with the general population of Fort Worth. The reason was mainly due to the fact that the dance hall was known to play "disreputable" music, including fiddle bands, hillbilly, and sometimes jazz. At the time, that same music was considered objectionable, not only in Fort Worth, but also nationwide. As the music slowly gained in acceptance, and as the Depression began, more individuals all across America sought the inexpensive entertainment of music and dancing. At Crystal Springs the dancing took place on an ample sized dance floor accommodating a few hundred dance couples. The building itself was not anywhere near opulent. It was a simple wooden building that had square wooden columns supporting the roof that were spaced about 20 feet apart down the center of the dance floor. Seating was limited to a few benches and tables were placed along the perimeter. But, as patron Fred Calhoun remembered, "Nobody ever sat down, though. They just stood up and danced" (Ginell, 117).

A major component of the increased popularity of dancing at Crystal Springs was the live music of Milton Brown and His Musical Brownies. Beginning about 1932 until his untimely death in 1936, Milton Brown reigned supreme at Crystal Springs. At first, the band played almost every night. As the popularity of the band increased, the overflow crowd often exceeded 800 to 1,000 people. Later, due to radio exposure, the Brownies toured other regional dance halls but continued to play Crystal Springs almost every Saturday night. On Saturday nights at Crystal Springs, the band began at 9:00 p.m. and played until 2:00 a.m., often without intermission. The Brownies were such an integral part of Crystal Springs that a 1934 promotional calendar for the dance hall featured the band. In December 1933, a "Season's Greetings from Milton Brown and the Musical Brownies" offered the following poem,

> If you would dance away your troubles,
> Live and laugh as ne'er before,
> See us at Crystal Springs more often
> Throughout 1934.

Music historian Cary Ginell added, "Milton Brown reigned over a small entertainment empire, whose subjects, for several hours each Saturday night, were oblivious to the outside world and the gnawing effects of the Depression" (115–117).

The "gnawing effects" were not only economic, but sometimes extreme hot or cold temperatures. Coal burning pot bellied stoves provided heat in the winter and ceiling fans provided some semblance of cooling in the summer. During the summer months a portion of the back wall was opened up to an adjoining outdoor pavilion, increasing

This Milton Brown and his Brownies record album advertised as a "Dance-O-Rama." Some of their western swing tunes on this album included "Right or Wrong" and the "Brownie Special." Also included was Brown's rendition of an early 1900 W. C. Handy classic, "St. Louis Blues." Brown's remake started out slow and increased to a faster tempo near the end. This song was such a crowd favorite that Brown often played the song at least twice each evening. (Author's Archives.)

the capacity to about 1,000 dancers. During the summer months the overflow dance crowd was also accommodated by the addition of an outdoor dance floor built over the swimming pool. Quite a few dancers combined dancing with a refreshing dip. Former patron Fred Calhoun remembered, "We used to go swimming after the dance on hot summer nights. Go right out back and dive in" (Ginell, 128).

Regional Touring

In late 1934 and into early 1935, the Musical Brownies shifted regular venues. The reason for the change was a disagreement over money. A short distance away from Crystal Springs, Brown invested in his own dance hall and named it the Brownie Tavern. The band also continued touring the region by bus. Milton's younger brother Roy Lee Brown remembered touring with the band during summer breaks from school. At first he was a "band boy" carrying equipment and changing guitar and fiddle strings. In August 1935, at 14 years of age, his first show was at a lodge hall in Palestine, Texas. Roy Lee recalled, "That's the first time I went with them to fix strings for [brother] Derwood." Their regional touring included other dance halls across Texas including, The Mineral Plunge in Waxahachie, and the Oak View Inn in Dennison. Not all the dance halls had names; in fact, many were converted community centers or picnic pavilions. Roy Lee also recalled a place "out in the country" that was somewhere "between Meridian and Rainsford Gap." The common factor among all, whether named or unnamed, was that all of the "places were for dancing" (Ginell, xxv; Thompson, "Interview").

The band usually played continuously and kept the crowd on the dance floor. Occasionally, an individual musician or two took a break while others in the band either played a long solo or a particular song that did not require all the instruments or vocals. For the most part, a long break or intermission without music usually led to an impatient crowd and sometimes fisticuffs. Roy Lee remembered, "Usually, if they took an intermission, fights would start. If you took the people who had danced and the ones that had drank, and the ones who danced AND drank, by 12 o'clock they were having a big time and they might be getting a chip on their shoulder and were ready to fight sometimes" (Ginell, 116–117).

In addition to The Mineral Plunge and the Oak View Inn, Roy Lee Brown recalled that the Brownies played "about 5 different places in Waco, [Texas]" but he could not remember the names. It was obvious that the Musical Brownies were the main draw and attracted a crowd wherever they played. During this same time the dance crowd abandoned Crystal Springs in favor of the Brownie Tavern. Business at Crystal Springs suffered and, combined with the economic hardship of the times, the hall almost closed. After a six-month hiatus, negotiations with Milton Brown brought his band back to Crystal Springs. Roy Lee Brown remembered, "Crystal Springs was a big dance hall. It could hold maybe eight or nine hundred people if you got them in just right. As dance halls go it wasn't really all that big, but to me, a little bitty kid, it looked tremendous" (Ginell, 116–117, 138).

A common factor among the many working bands that played the dance halls of the Southwest was that they did not play many new or original songs. For the most part, the rural inhabitants who attended the Saturday night dances wanted to hear either radio "hits," old favorites, or songs from their homeland. The forte of bands such as the Musical Brownies was listening to the radio and covering some of the "pop" radio hits of the day. Brown's signature opening number, "About a Quarter to Nine," for example, was a song that he had first heard on the radio and one that was also featured in a Hollywood movie. During the 1930s, as a singer, or more appropriately as a "Hillbilly" singer as he was called at the time, Brown's vocal talents blended contemporary jazz styling similar with contemporaries Ted Lewis and Cab Calloway. Yet at a time when string and fiddle bands were mainly instrumental, Brown changed the nucleus of the instrumental to focus on the vocals. A change that biographer Cary Ginell called "revolutionary to Texas rural music" (xxi).

Another crowd favorite was Brown's slow-tempo rendition of an early 1900 classic of W. C. Handy's "St. Louis Blues." The song was one that he had first performed with the Wills Fiddle Band. The old ragtime tune allowed couples to do the slow drag or the Country & Western "Buckle Polisher." Brown did add a twist to "St. Louis Blues" as he often instructed the band to play at a slow tempo for well over 10 and sometimes 20 minutes. Near the end of the song he increased to a faster tempo. "St. Louis Blues" became such a crowd favorite that Brown often played the song at least twice each evening. Each time, the crowd anxiously awaited the tempo change. When Brown recorded his version for Decca Records, it was condensed to three minutes, but the tempo change remained intact. During every performance throughout the four to five hours of continuous dance music, Brown also varied fast-paced Polkas and Two Steps mixed with slower tempo Waltz and ballad tunes. Fortunately for the dancers, but not always welcomed by the exhausted musicians, the long stretches of music were also welcomed by the management. Dancing kept everyone happy and occupied (Ginell, 130–132).

Crystal Springs drew entire families, young and old, as did almost all the other rural southwestern dance halls. The band focused on music for dancing, but many people also went just to listen to the music. In fact, most of the rural dance halls also admitted families with children of all ages. Sometimes the children would watch the dancing and try to emulate their parents. Others might run around and play outside. When the children were tired or sleepy, it was not unusual to find them sleeping on wooden tables that were usually scattered about both inside and outside just about any rural dance hall.

Segregation and the "One Drop Rule"

Sadly though, with very few exceptions the dance halls throughout America were strictly segregated by the color of skin. This was not only limited to the dance halls. Segregation, often specifically written into law, extended to all places of public accommodation, strictly separating whites from "Negroes." In the southern states from coast to coast and also up through the Midwest, state legislatures enacted laws mandating that any American citizen who had at least "one-drop of non-white blood" be officially classified as a "Negro." In 1910, Tennessee and Louisiana were the first states to officially pass into law what became known as the "one drop rule." The following year Arkansas and Texas did the same, and Mississippi did so in 1917. After a brief respite, mainly due to American involvement in World War I, North Carolina ratified the "one-drop" law in 1923, as did Virginia in 1924, designating the law the Virginia Racial Integrity Act. Alabama and Georgia followed suit with similar laws in 1927, as did Oklahoma in 1931. Shortly thereafter, in quick succession, other states including Florida, Indiana, Kentucky, Maryland, Missouri, Nebraska, North Dakota, and Utah revised their pre-existing laws to strengthen the "one-drop" rule. The Ku Klux Klan, either through fear placed upon "non-whites," or by physical beatings or lynching, usually maintained enforcement of these laws. Regardless of the Klan, by 1925, all of the 48 states had either a law or a statute defining a person with at least "one drop" of non-white blood as a "colored person." In turn, separation of whites and Negroes, especially during dancing, was strictly enforced (Giordano 2007, 108, 110–111).

Amplification and the Dust Bowl

During the Depression economic times were tough, but most people, both white and non-white, sought the inexpensive diversion of dancing. In response, during the mid-1930s, the federally funded Works Progress Administration (WPA) sponsored numerous free entertainment programs and music for dancing. The WPA also built community halls specifically for recreation and dancing. One example was located in Caldwell, Idaho, and in addition to Saturday evening dances also showed movies, provided sewing classes and children's activities, and contained a library. Many of the WPA programs extended into all areas across America. Almost all of them provided free dancing both in urban parks and rural areas. The social dancing included the Lindy Hop, Fox Trot, and other contemporary round dances as well as folk dancing, square dancing, polka, waltzes, old-time schottisches, and Country & Western.

In addition to sponsorship, WPA federal funding also built dedicated dance halls and ballrooms. Some WPA dance halls were actually open air dance halls and some, such as those in Utah, did not have a roof, in keeping with Mormon culture. Two such examples were the Rooftop Gardens in Midvale, Utah, which was actually built upon a flat roof above a Mormon Church, and an outdoor dance hall in Sanpete County that was built on the edge of a mountain ridge. Other outdoor dance pavilions, built with roofs, in neighboring non-Mormon communities, had names such as The Rendezvous, The Purple Haze, and The Starlight. The WPA also built permanent ballrooms in almost all the cities and rural areas throughout the country. One example was Glen Echo Park in Maryland, which opened in 1933, and Schuyler's Oak Ballroom in Nebraska, which opened in 1936.

During the same time, less than 10 percent of rural areas had access to electricity. Fuel generators often powered the lighting and rudimentary sound systems of the regional dance halls. It was not unusual for the generator either to malfunction or run out of fuel. Patrons were accustomed to an occasional power failure and an unexpected break from dancing of 10 or 20 minutes while the generator was refueled. Despite the lack of electrical power, the amplification and sound systems for the bands were rudimentary at best. As for the Musical Brownies, Roy Lee Brown said, "They had two speakers, one amplifier, and one microphone." The one microphone was for the vocalist and the fiddle players who stood on either side of Milton and close to the microphone. When it was time for a fiddle solo or highlight, the vocalist would step aside and the fiddler would step closer to the microphone. During the course of the evening, Roy Lee explained, "That way they could move back or forth and could step up closer to the mike as needed." In some cases an individual player would tote along their own amplifier. In the Musical Brownies, steel guitar player Bob Dunn had his own Volu-Tone brand amplifier. Dunn is most often attributed as having the first amplified steel guitar in a Country & Western band (Pfeffer, "Western Swing Bands History").

Milton Brown continually sought out musical innovation such as Dunn's lap steel guitar. Other innovations in the Musical Brownies included the addition of an upright string bass. Similar to some other string bands, they also added twin fiddles and a piano. The piano was an essential instrument for many of the touring bands, but very few traveled with one and therefore relied on whether or not the dance hall had a piano. More often than not, a piano would be in place, but it was usually "broken down" and almost always out of tune (Thompson, "Interview with Roy Lee Brown—Part 2").

In addition to the lack of power and the nationwide economic depression, the rural Southwest and up through the Midwest were especially hard hit from 1932 through 1934. Areas such as Texas, Oklahoma, Kansas, Nebraska, South Dakota, and North Dakota experienced an environmental disaster that came to be known as the Dust Bowl. The harsh hot summer months were unusually dry, as almost no rainfall caused severe drought conditions. The severe lack of rainfall caused the ground to dry up and in many instances induced fissure cracks; in turn the topsoil literally blew away in the wind. Farmers were devastated, and many farm owners and migrant workers simply packed up their belongings and moved west in search of work and better conditions. Some estimates placed the displacement to California, Washington, and Oregon at about 2.5 million people.

In response to the problems, the federally funded WPA began two massive construction projects: the Hoover Dam and a series of dams known as the Tennessee Valley Authority. Both projects sought to provide irrigation to alleviate the dust bowl problem, and also to provide a source of hydroelectric power. Under the auspices of the Rural Electrification Administration (REA) power lines connected about 40 percent of all homes and businesses in rural areas with access to electrical power. The availability of electricity also brought an increase in radio ownership and access to news, sports, drama, and, of course, music of all kinds (Giordano 2003, 85).

As a result, radio stations such as WSM's Grand Ole Opry from Nashville and Chicago's WLS National Barn Dance popularized "Hillbilly" music with the focus on dancing. With the genre of Hillbilly music so distinct, the Musical Brownies seemed a peculiar hybrid that could not necessarily be easily labeled as Hillbilly, Jazz, or Pop. Therefore, the Brownies were mostly ignored by radio stations, but not by the dancers.

Unfortunately, in April 1936, Milton Brown's growing reputation was sadly cut short by a fatal car accident just outside of Crystal

Springs. Brown was severely injured and died a few days later. After his death, dancing continued at Crystal Springs with a new regular band named the Crystal Springs Ramblers. The Musical Brownies continued after Brown's death led by brother Derwood; but by mid-1937, they disbanded. At the time of Brown's death, there were many other bands touring the regional dance halls, honky-tonks, roadhouses, and county fairs. Some, such as Adolph Hofner, played Polkas and Schottisches catering to German immigrants. Others playing Country & Western included Hank Penny and the Prairie Ramblers, Jimmy Revard and the Oklahoma Playboys, Texas Jim Lewis and His Lone Star Cowboys, Bill Boyd's Cowboy Ramblers, The Tune Wranglers, The Southern Melody Boys, and the Western Swing of Bob Wills and the Texas Playboys (Ginell, xxi, 136).

Swing Music and the Big Bands of the 1930s

By the mid-1930s, dancing of all styles was a widely popular entertainment all across America. Many younger Americans jitterbugged to the big band sounds of swing music typified by the likes of Cab Calloway, Duke Ellington, the Casa Loma Orchestra, and Benny Goodman, among hundreds of others. Older adults danced the Fox Trot, Waltz, and Rumba to music played by orchestras led by Wayne King, Guy Lombardo, Vincent Lopez, Fred Warring, and Paul Whiteman, among hundreds of others. The big bands were typically noted as appealing to urban areas and big cities such as Detroit, Los Angeles, Chicago, and New York. Although the music and dance styles were obviously somewhat divided by age, they also differed greatly between urban and rural areas.

A noticeable difference in the big bands of the 1930s from the bands of previous years was the addition of multiple horn sections and a change in some of the stringed instruments. The banjo, for example, was a prominent instrument in the ragtime and jazz bands of the 1910s and 1920s, but in the big bands it was replaced by the guitar. On the other hand the banjo was often found in a 1930s Country & Western southwestern string band, as was the guitar. The southwestern style was based heavily upon stringed instruments, dominated by the fiddle, whereas the big bands were dominated by multiple brass instruments. A stand-up string bass replaced the tuba from the jazz bands and was also incorporated in the Country & Western bands.

For the big bands, it was the change in instruments that allowed the music to "swing."

The musical style of swing, however, was always difficult to describe. In fact, a band could play the same number night after night and sometimes the musicians felt the music "swing" while other times they knew it just did not "swing." In turn, the dancers usually noticed the same result. In his biography *The Kingdom of Swing*, famed bandleader Benny Goodman offered a simple analogy to describe swing. He explained,

> Those who have asked for a one-word or one-sentence definition of swing overlook the fact that it was originally a term used among musicians to identify something they all recognized. How, for example, would you describe *red* for a child, who did not know what it was? You would point to something that was red, and say: "That is red." ... Similarly with swing—it can be identified in an actual performance or on a record, and then recognized when it recurs in another performance, but it cannot be defined as a component of such and such elements. In a word, swing is a property of music played in a certain way, rather than a definite kind of music itself. (174)

It was Benny Goodman, dubbed the King of Swing, who was often credited as the musician who set the pattern for the great dance bands of the period and for bringing swing into national prominence.

During early 1935, as Benny Goodman and his orchestra toured the country, swing music was not overly popular beyond the nation's teenagers. However, after almost one year on the road, Goodman combined a successful tour in Los Angeles attended by 2,500 enthusiastic dancers with a four-week, sold-out stay in Chicago. As a result, national attention by major newspapers and national media magazines promoted not only Goodman, but also swing music and jitterbugging as a national phenomenon. Soon thereafter, swing music and dancing the Jitterbug (a simpler version of the Lindy Hop) caught on nationwide, even in the southwestern rural areas. Music historian Ernie Smith noted that the Lindy Hop and the Jitterbug "was immensely popular with regional dancers." Not only was Lindy Hop and Jitterbug dancing popular in the Southwest, the music was also influential among other musical styles. In the case of Bob Wills and the Texas Playboys, their music was also swing. By the end of the 1930s, mainly as a result of the influence of swing music applied by both Wills and Milton Brown, the standard fare of Country & Western dancing

From 1934 until 1943, Bob Wills and The Texas Playboys played regular dances at Cain's Ballroom in Tulsa, Oklahoma. This photo was taken during the 1970s. (Photograph by and used by permission of Richard Galbraith.)

included, according to music historian Ernie Smith, "a lively mixture of traditional country square dancing, ballroom, the Fox Trot, and . . . the addition of the Lindy Hop" (Miler and Jensen 1996, xx).

The Texas Playboys Swinging at Cain's Ballroom

At the time that Milton and Derwood Brown left The Light Crust Doughboys, Bob Wills was still a member of the Burrus Mill sponsored band. However, in 1933, Wills also had a disagreement with general manager "Pappy" O'Daniel. In all likelihood, the issue was over the same monetary issues that Milton and Derwood had the previous year. As a result of the disagreement, O'Daniel fired Wills from the band. Undaunted, Wills formed his own band, naming them "Bob Wills and The Texas Playboys," and moved to Tulsa, Oklahoma. Some sources indicate the relocation to Oklahoma was the result of O'Daniel's influence that blackballed Wills in the state of Texas.

Nonetheless, by February 1934, Wills secured a daily radio spot on KVOO radio in Tulsa, Oklahoma. On Saturday evenings a live remote radio show was broadcast from Cain's Ballroom, also in Tulsa.

From 1934 until 1943, Bob Wills and The Texas Playboys played regular dances at Cain's and also continued the live radio show. Although the broadcast from Cain's ended in 1943, Wills and his band continued the KVOO radio program until 1958. Similar to the Musical Brownies, the popular radio program created a demand for the Texas Playboys to travel to other regional dance halls. Similar to the Musical Brownies, the daily radio program made traveling to other shows and back quite hectic. Wills did not necessarily knock the hard life on the road. In later years in a recorded interview regarding the touring he said, "It's a lot of fun to play a dance, jump in our cars, drive three or four hundred miles and sleep an hour or two and go play another

As the band increased in popularity, Bob Wills and the Texas Playboys traveled throughout the region playing one dance hall after another, sometimes as far as 500 miles apart. At first they traveled by car, but in later years, as shown here, they purchased a touring bus emblazoned with the name of the band. In this promotional photo the cowboys and horses were added for effect, but obviously did not travel with the band. Wills is on the horse on the right in this photo taken in October of 1945 in Fresno, California. (Photo by Frank Driggs/Michael Ochs Archives/Getty Images, Editorial Image No. 74934599.)

dance and drive another 500 miles." Later on, they abandoned their cars and bought a touring bus (Liner notes, *Ride with Bob!!*, 4).

The main ingredient of the music of Bob Wills and The Texas Playboys was a hybrid of swing and traditional country music. The simple unifying theme, regardless of the influence, was that Wills's music, according to biographer Charles R. Townsend, was "always primarily for dancing." In fact, this was the main ingredient, combining both swing and traditional country music, with the emphasis always on dancing, that set Wills's music apart from the distinctive budding country music sound of the southeastern portion of the United States. Although both the music of the Southeast and Southwest emerged from the same basic ethnic and folk roots, there was a difference. Texas Playboy member Leon McAuliffe described it as,

> The basic difference in country and western music, if there is any way of defining it, is that west of the Mississippi River when we played, we played for dancing. East of the Mississippi they played a show, or they played in a schoolhouse, just for people to sit and listen, visual or audible entertainment and not for dancing. (Townsend, 38)

In an interview years later, Wills described his own musical style: "It was rhythmic, infectious music designed for dancing" (Casey, 43).

Bob Wills's "unusually danceable" music was often attributed to a musical style of syncopated phrasing and an upbeat rhythm. One western swing bandleader, Ted Daffan of Houston, described it as follows, "What Bob Wills did was take a heavy-accented two-beat, come in on it slightly early, and lay on the intricate rhythms in between" (Chadwick, "The Two Step"). A major factor contributing to the "rhythm" was Wills's use of horns and drums. Unlike the string bands of the other southwestern bands, Wills introduced drums in his band. Drums were so non-country that even during later shows at the fabled Grand Ole Opry during the 1960s and 1970s, drums were not allowed on stage. In rare instances at the Grand Ole Opry, when drums were part of the band such as The Texas Playboys, the drummer was usually located offstage or behind a curtain (Ginell, xxx).

In a similar manner, the rhythm and horns employed by the Texas Playboys were a bit different from other traditional country string bands. Their main influences were the contemporary big band sounds such as Benny Goodman, Glenn Miller, and Tommy Dorsey, among others. Texas Playboy band member Leon McAuliffe reiterated, "Our music was never country music. . . . *Country and western* [italics in original] is an inappropriate term, in my opinion. I can't think of a country artist we ever listened to and learned their tunes. We listened to Benny Goodman, Glenn Miller, Louis Armstrong, and (Bob) Crosby" (Townsend, 285).

Many of the songs played by The Texas Playboys were remakes of old standards, including the blues song, "Trouble On My Mind," a 1920s jazz classic, "Basin Street Blues," a ragtime favorite, "Steel Guitar Rag," and a cover of the pre-1920 Irving Berlin classic, "Alexander's Rag Time Band." Regardless of the genre, Wills adapted all the songs to his style of swing, but also maintained some of their original sound. Some traditional favorites and originals were "Cotton-Eyed Joe," "Ida Red," "San Antonio Rose," and "Take Me Back to Tulsa." Eventually, the Texas Playboys had a large repertoire of both old songs and original material. In a later interview Wills said, "You can change the name of an old song, rearrange it and make it swing" (Casey, 43).

In later years, Wills's title as the King of Western Swing came mainly due to his longevity. In comparison, by the time Wills and the Texas Playboys made their first recordings in 1935, Milton Brown and the Musical Brownies had recorded over 50 of their eventual 102 songs at sessions in both San Antonio and Chicago. During the 1940s, as Wills grew in popularity, he changed the name of the band to Bob Wills and His Texas Playboys. Nonetheless, Wills's songs and music were greatly influential and were recorded by many other musical artists through the 20th- and well into the 21st century. Nevertheless, in an interview in 1949, Wills remembered his early success was based on one simple formula. He said, "We was just tryin' to find enough tunes to keep 'em dancin' " (Townsend, "Homecoming").

2

Honky Tonks
and Dance Halls

"No doubt about it. They come here to dance."
—Joe Thibodeaux, owner of the Rodair Club

In August 1945, World War II ended dramatically with the dropping of atomic bombs on Hiroshima and Nagasaki. (The victory in Europe had ended a few months earlier.) Although much of the world was literally in ruins, mainland America was relatively intact. Within a short time, over 12 million American servicemen and women were shipped back to the United States in the hope of living in postwar peace and prosperity. For many, the availability of the G. I. Bill allowed veterans the opportunity for college educational tuition waivers, job training, and a Veterans Administration 30-year home mortgage to purchase their own home, among other benefits. Within the first year of the end of the war, over 3 million women left the workforce and became newly married or reunited with soldier-husbands. Birth rates increased dramatically, and the baby boom began. Within the postwar period, many strived for a newly idealized "American Dream" of home ownership, marriage, family, and consumerism—a dream that was continually portrayed in television and other mass-market media such as magazines and newspapers.

During those years, Americans had to contend with the new "Cold War" with the Soviet Union, as a U.S. foreign policy of the containment of Communism was first and foremost in the minds of all Americans.

By 1950, a widespread paranoia that engulfed the entire country became known as the "red-scare," as Senator Joseph McCarthy and the House Un-American Activities Committee (HUAC) seized the newspaper headlines, falsely warning Americans that they were endangered by Communist infiltration in Hollywood and government. McCarthy's false warnings were taken quite seriously, and hundreds of thousands of adults built backyard underground bomb shelters to protect themselves in case of a nuclear attack. During this scare, schoolchildren were taught to "stop, drop, and cover" as they actively participated in Civil Defense drills.

The schools—and also the nation—were hatefully divided by legal segregation, although this was gradually dismantled as individuals such as baseball players Jackie Robinson in the National League and Larry Doby in the American League broke the color barrier in 1947; and Rosa Parks refused to give up her seat on a bus in Montgomery, Alabama in 1955. The previous year, the U.S. Supreme Court in the *Brown vs. the Board of Education* decision effectively ended nationwide school segregation. Within that politically and socially charged climate, Rock 'n' Roll music exploded upon the American scene. Many of the artists, such as Chuck Berry, Little Richard, and Fats Domino, had roots in Rhythm and Blues. Others, including Elvis Presley, Buddy Holly, Jerry Lee Lewis, Carl Perkins, and Bill Haley and the Comets, had their roots in Country & Western music.

Square Dancing and Hollywood Cowboys

During World War II, American soldiers from all over the nation received basic training in camps located in Nebraska, Oklahoma, and Texas, and other states. Recreation and USO shows were an integral part of military life and often included Saturday night dances. In many cases, the soldiers danced to the very popular big band swing music of the likes of Glenn Miller and Benny Goodman. In many other areas, however, it was often Country & Western music and sometimes accompanied by square dancing. The term "square dancing" in itself is often a wrongly applied term to just about any form of traditional American folk dancing, including Country & Western. The application might well have been traced to the early American colonial days of the French Contredanse and English Country-dances. These were danced in a myriad of set figures, patterns, and round dances. As time progressed and other dances, such as the Waltz and Polka, were introduced in the eastern formal ballrooms, the Country-dances were more often relegated to rural areas. During the late 19th and the first half of the 20th century they were also found in small towns and at barn dances.

In these locations, attendees also heard Country & Western music and Western Swing. Therefore, it is quite possible that those who were unfamiliar with the style could not distinguish between square dancing and the round dances of Country & Western. That misconception was reinforced by some popular Hollywood movies. In 1941, for example, the comedy team of Abbott and Costello, who were known nationwide, featured a square dance scene in a barn in the movie *Ride 'Em Cowboy.*

Throughout the war, military personnel were also exposed to the music of Western Swing while stationed in Venice, California. At the time, the west coast was abuzz with wartime activity, including war production plants and military base locations for shipping sailors and soldiers to the South Pacific. The area attracted hundreds of thousands in search of work, some dating back to the 1930s when migrants from the Southwest were forced to leave their native states of Texas, Oklahoma, Nebraska; and others due to the environmental disaster of the Dust Bowl. As they settled in southern California in search of work, these immigrants brought along their meager possessions which included fiddles, guitars, and the music of the Southwest. Later, during World War II, similar workers from all areas of the Midwest and Southwest migrated to both the east coast and west coast seeking employment in war industry related jobs. As World War II progressed, Bob Wills and the Texas Playboys continued playing Western Swing and even brought it to California. Western Swing historian Cary Ginell suggested that a major reason for Wills's relocation to California was to further his movie career. His appearance in Hollywood movies such as *Go West, Young Lady* (1941) and *Take Me Back to Oklahoma* (1940) introduced Western Swing music to an audience well beyond the range of any 50,000-watt Southwest radio station (Ginell, xxvi).

In these heavily over-populated areas, both the workers and military personnel sought recreation, many of them through music and dancing. In Venice, California, for example, the bands that played Western Swing, such as Wills's, often attracted dancers who were quite familiar with the big bands and jitterbugging. In response to the music, Ginell noted, there was "top-notch jitterbugging, jumping around, cutting loose and going crazy" (xxvi). During the 1940s and into the 1950s, Western Swing music drew large crowds in and around Venice and the Los Angeles area. Some of the most well-known clubs that were home to popular Western Swing bands included the Venice Pier Ballroom, the Riverside Rancho in Los Feliz, and the Santa Monica Ballroom.

By the late 1940s, however, a square dance movement throughout the United States overshadowed traditional Country & Western dancing. Many of the nation's schools provided square dancing in their physical education programs. Community centers, YMCAs, and other organizations also promoted it as a healthy recreation activity. In a short time, people young and old all over the country were enjoying square dancing. Square dance festivals and barn dances were held in towns of every size, including large cities such as New York, attracting between 5,000 and 10,000 participants. In addition, Hollywood capitalized on that popularity with *Hollywood Barn Dance* (1947), *Square Dance Jubilee* (1949), *The Arkansas Swing* (1949), and *Square Dance Katy* (1950). By the 1950s, there was also a proliferation of movie westerns dating from a trend that began in the 1930s. A popular movie format was a "singing cowboy." The combination of the singing cowboy, barn dances, and western swing music became quite a popular trend in postwar Hollywood movies.

The Singing Cowboys and Eddy Arnold

Many in the mainstream American public associated Country & Western music only with what they saw in Hollywood movies. Dating from the 1930s through the 1950s, movie westerns were a profitable Hollywood venture. Some of the movies featured singing cowboys of the likes of Roy Rogers, Gene Autry, and the Sons of the Pioneers. Prior to his solo career, Rogers was a member of the Sons of the Pioneers. With Rogers in the cast, and even after he had left, the Sons of the Pioneers appeared in over 80 movie westerns between the years 1935 and 1948. The group perfected a distinct three-part harmony that was widely copied in all genres of music (Lomax, "Country Music").

Rogers' first starring cowboy role was a 1938 feature film, *Under Western Stars*, and a short time thereafter he was a major western movie star. Between 1938 and 1953, he appeared in over 100 films and shorts.

He later moved on to a very popular television series; and a generation of Baby Boomers grew up watching his weekly half-hour TV show with his wife Dale Evans and his horse Trigger. It was during the post-war period that Rogers befriended musician Spade Cooley, who bore a striking resemblance to him. Cooley had auditioned as a stand-in and stunt double for Rogers, and they soon became friends. As for Roy Rogers, many of those born after the 1970s simply remember him as the founder and co-owner of a restaurant chain bearing his name (Lomax, "Cowboy Music").

Gene Autry, on the other hand, was probably the most famous and definitely the most financially successful of all the Hollywood singing cowboys. In 1929, Autry began some early recordings on various publishing labels including Victor, Okeh, and Columbia Records, patterning his singing after the smooth, country crooning style of Jimmie Rodgers. In 1930, Autry billed himself as "Oklahoma's Singing Cowboy" and earned a spot on the KVOO radio station in Tulsa. The following year, his release of "Silver Haired Daddy of Mine," (which he co-wrote with Jimmy Long) sold an astonishing five million copies. Shortly thereafter, Autry garnered a regular radio spot on the *WLS Barn Dance* program for Chicago. His success earned him an uncredited role in the Ken Maynard movie, *In Old Santa Fe* (1934). His performance was good enough to earn him a starring role in a serial short, *The Phantom Empire* (1935). In quick succession, Autry and his horse Champion appeared in many Hollywood B movie westerns as both he and his horse were likeable celebrities throughout America.

As for his music, Autry was definitely one of the most successful and popular singers of his era. He piled up hit after hit, including "Yellow Rose of Texas" in 1933, followed in successive years by "The Last Roundup," "Tumbling Tumbleweeds," and "Mexicali Rose." In 1939 "Back In The Saddle Again" put him back at the top of the charts, as did "South Of The Border" in 1940, and three big hits in 1941: "You Are My Sunshine," "It Makes No Difference Now," and "Be Honest With Me." In 1942, "Tweedle-O-Twill" hit the top of the charts as did the 1945 wartime themed song, "At Mail Call Today." In later years, Autry was the majority owner of the California Angels baseball team. Of all Autry's accomplishments and song hits, none were more memorable than the endearing Christmas classic of his 1948 rendition of "Rudolph the Red-Nosed Reindeer." The song sold over nine million copies and was played year-after-year every Christmas all across America well into the 21st century ("Cowboy Music").

But Country & Western music did in fact achieve significant airplay without the aid of movies. One of the most notable singers of the post-war period was Eddy Arnold. In a 2008 *New York Times* obituary, Arnold (1918–2008) was described as a singer who "personified the evolution of country music in the years after World War II from a rural vernacular to an idiom with broad mainstream appeal." In the mid-1930s, at the age of 18 he began playing guitar and appearing in local saloons. In 1940, he joined as lead singer with Pee Wee King's Golden West Cowboys, often appearing at the Grand Ole Opry. A few years later he left to form his own group, the Tennessee Plowboys. Soon thereafter, he launched an unparalleled recording career.

In a recording career that spanned seven decades, Eddy Arnold sold over 85 million records. During his lifetime, he also held the distinction of having his singles on the country music charts occupy "more time at the top" combined than any other country music artist. Thirty-seven of his hit country songs crossed over onto the mainstream pop charts, including his signature hit song "Make the World Go Away" during the fall of 1965. At the time, it played alongside the songs by the British Invasion groups, including the Beatles, the Rolling Stones, Herman's Hermits, as well as the Motown hits of the Supremes and the Tempta-tions. Arnold's biggest success, however, came in the immediate post-war years of 1945 to 1954. During that time, Arnold had 57 consecutive singles place in the Country & Western Top 10. Nineteen of those hits also reached #1. Two of his hit songs from that time, "I'll Hold You in My Heart (Till I Can Hold You in My Arms)" and "I Wanna Play House With You," were later recorded by Elvis Presley, who also made them hits. In fact, Arnold's manager during that string of 57 hits was Col. Tom Parker, who later went on to manage Presley, a pioneer of Rock 'n' Roll.

Arnold, on the other hand, stayed away from Rock 'n' Roll songs. Faced with a changing music industry that was embracing Rock 'n' Roll during the 1950s and later the sounds of the Beatles during the 1960s, Arnold often appeared in a tuxedo and sang ballads, backed by an orches-tra with strings. His new image as a "cabaret-style singer" was described by one reviewer as "the embodiment of hillbilly music's move from the country to the city." Arnold himself said,

I've never thought of myself as a country-and-western singer. With the type of material I do, I'm really a pop music artist. . . . I want my songs to be accepted by everybody.

Arnold's songs certainly appealed to a more diverse mainstream audience, but he was personified by his post-World War II years and Country & Western music. At that same time, Western Swing also garnered a wider audience (Friskics-Warren, "Eddy Arnold," C11).

Another similar band of the time was "Texas Jim" Lewis and the Lone Star Cowboys. Jim Lewis (1909–1990) began playing in bands with his brother Jack during the early 1930s in Houston, Texas. A few years later he joined Jack West and his Circle Star Cowboys in Detroit, Michigan, often playing on a radio show on local station WJR. In the late 1930s, Lewis left the Circle Star Cowboys to form his own Lone Star Cowboys. Much of their work was in and around New York City. In 1937, they joined the ranks of Hollywood cowboy bands, appearing in the movie *Drug Store Follies* (1937). Lewis and his band appeared in 10 other feature films and short movies. In each, he played himself, as did the members of the Lone Star Cowboys. The movies included, *All Aboard* (1937), *Swingin' in the Barn* (1940), *Bad Man from Red Butte* (1940), *Down Mexico Way* (1941), *Pardon My Gun* (1942), and *The Old Homestead* (1942), among a few others. In 1944, Lewis and the Lone Star Cowboys scored with one of the biggest hit songs of the 1940s, "Too Late To Worry, Too Blue To Cry." By that time, Lewis and a few of the band members had been drafted into the armed services. The remaining members recruited new musicians and Lewis was replaced as the front man by Spade Cooley. After the war, Lewis started a new band in California and eventually headed to the Northwest and Seattle, Washington. In Seattle, Lewis had his own radio program and soon thereafter a local television cowboy show named *Ranier Ranch*. From 1950 to 1957, he concentrated solely on television. In 1960, he re-formed his Western Swing band, continuing to play local venues well into the 1970s (Pfeffer, "Western Swing Bands History").

Spade Cooley, the King of Western Swing

Although the musical style as played by the likes of Bob Wills and Milton Brown was Western Swing, it was not officially named until the 1940s. And it was Spade Cooley who is most often credited with naming it "Western Swing." Clyde Donnell "Spade" Cooley (1910–1969) was born near rural Pack Saddle Creek in Oklahoma. Possibly in response to the Dust Bowl, but certainly due to the hard economic times, the Cooley family moved to Modesto, California. He searched for work in the southern California area and found many of the migrant workers eager to hear the sounds of the Southwest. Music historian Jean A. Boyd in *The Jazz of the Southwest* said, "The music these people had known and loved back home was played in numerous dance halls and clubs, which provided a great deal of work for musicians" (25). Cooley, to his credit, reintroduced the fiddle as the driving force in his band. With sometimes three or more fiddles combined with steel guitar, and later the new electric guitar, he replaced and basically eliminated all the horns from his music. At the time, Cooley's manger tried an advertising phrase and billed him, "Spade Cooley, King of Western Swing." The naming of the music style was closely associated with Cooley's large popularity at the Ventura Ballroom and also in Hollywood. In 1945, Warner Bros. Pictures released a 10-minute short, *Spade Cooley King of Western Swing*, which Cooley built on during his self-promotion of the title. By the 1940s, the label stuck and Coley's music was known as "Western Swing."

But, by 1946, Cooley's "Western Swing band" catered to the diverse dancing crowd by playing Rumbas, Boogie Woogie, and Blues, among other popular musical styles. Boyd explained, "After the war, Spade Cooley (in Los Angeles) introduced a variant of western swing that deemphasized the brass and reeds while returning to the more traditional sound of pop orchestras" (25–26). As a result, his popularity continued upward, but almost exclusively west of the Mississippi, and especially in southern California where Cooley was well-known. He amassed a small fortune from musical appearances at the Ventura Ballroom, Hollywood movies, and a long-running television show. Cooley was a pioneer in the early days of broadcasting, as he starred his own TV show. In 1947, Cooley went on the air beginning a successful six-year run with *The Spade Cooley Show*. One report noted that of the 1.5 million TV sets in southern California at the time, at least 1.3 million were regularly tuned into Cooley's Saturday evening show. During that time, Cooley also wrote music and appeared in Hollywood movies. Throughout the 1950s, his prosperity and innovative ideas continued as he prepared plans for a large amusement theme park in the Mojave Desert (Boyd, 27).

On April 3, 1961, however, Cooley's career suddenly ended as he was jailed for the murder of his wife. Apparently, Cooley physically beat his wife to death in a jealous rage. (Cooley, who had a long history of domestic violence, accused her of having an affair with Roy Rogers.) The trial attracted national media attention as the headlines proclaimed that Cooley's murder took place in front of their daughter Melody, who later testified in court. He was sentenced to a 25-year prison term, but after a little more than eight years he was paroled. Within days of his release he suffered a massive heart attack and died while still in prison (Pfeffer, "Western Swing Bands History").

Spade Cooley certainly had a life of ongoing troubles, but disagreements with his band members had started almost immediately. Shortly after the war, musician Tex Williams and others left Cooley's band and set out on their own. Some sources indicated that they left in disagreement of Cooley's divergence from traditional Country & Western roots, especially with the Hollywood productions. Williams, for one, continued fronting a nine-member Country & Western swing band

The musical style played by Bob Wills and Milton Brown was Western Swing, but it was not officially named until the 1940s, and credited to Spade Cooley. In this 1940 photo, Spade Cooley is seen standing in front near the piano and holding a fiddle. His orchestra is dressed in the standard cowboy and cowgirl fashion featured in Hollywood movies of the time. (Photo by Frank Driggs Collection/Getty Images, Editorial image No. 50916062.)

collective known as the Western Caravan. The Western Caravan stayed true to the tradition of Western Swing as played by Bob Wills and Milton Brown. The band included the traditional arrangement of a pair of guitars and twin fiddles along with a stand-up bass, electric steel lap guitar, vibes, accordion, and drums. Most of the band's work centered in and around the Los Angeles area, oftentimes at a sold-out Roller Rink on Glendale Boulevard in Los Angeles (Erlewine, "Milton Brown").

Hank Williams and The Grand Ole Opry

Despite his tragic ending, Cooley's musical influence, along with the influence of Bob Wills and Milton Brown, laid the groundwork for many others in Country & Western. Other contemporaries of Cooley included Lefty Frizzell, Ernest Tubb, Hank Thompson, Faron Young, and Hank Williams. Although those artists had achieved distinction as marketable radio singers, they played music mainly for dancing. During that time, Country & Western music was often associated with dancing and the Grand Ole Opry in Nashville, Tennessee. The publicity was the result of live Saturday night broadcasts of Country & Western music artists by WSM radio since 1925.

Affectionately known simply as "The Opry," it developed its name as it went on-air following an opera program. Originally titled the *WSM Barn Dance* as it was broadcast from 1925 to 1927, the show acquired its lasting name from an announcer's introduction that went as follows, "For the past hour we have been listening to music taken largely from grand opera, but from now on we will present the Grand Ole Opry." By 1939, the Opry joined as part of the national network of the National Broadcasting Company (NBC). That national attention was often credited to the addition of Roy Acuff as host. By 1959, the Grand Ole Opry was ranked the favorite radio show in all of America (Sandow, "Grand Ole Opry").

Not as widely well-known to history, but also very popular during its time was WWVA's Country Jamboree. This live radio show was broadcast on WWVA at 1170AM on the radio dial from the 2,400-seat Capitol Music Hall Theater in Wheeling, West Virginia for 72 years— ending its fabled run in 2005. During its prime, the show attracted "hundreds of thousands of country music fans" to Wheeling each year. The show also had its share of country music stars including such nationally known singers as Johnny Cash, Charley Pride, and Merle Haggard, among others. Throughout its run, it was "the second-longest-running live country music show" behind the Grand Ole Opry (Hamill, "A City Sees Its Past," A13).

Much of the success of the Grand Ole Opry was attributed to musician and entrepreneur Roy Acuff. In 1933, Acuff formed a group known as the Tennessee Crackerjacks playing through the Southeast and Southwest. In 1938, he made his first appearance on the Opry. Soon thereafter, he changed the name of the band to the Smoky Mountain Boys and they became regulars on the show. Some of Acuff's biggest hits were recorded during World War II and were popular among members of the armed services, at USO dances, as well as on WSM radio. They included, "Wreck on the Highway," "Fireball Mail," "Night Train to Memphis," "Tied Down," "That's What Makes the Jukebox Play," and "The Precious Jewel." Shortly after the war, Acuff bought the rights to the enormously popular adult and later children's classic song and dance the "Hokey Pokey." His Acuff-Rose record label made a small fortune from that song alone. Acuff remained popular on the Grand Ole Opry until his death in 1992 (Roughstock's, "Acuff & the Grand Ole Opry").

At the time, music was divided into three basic categories: Popular, Country & Western, and Rhythm & Blues. (The previous year, the three charts were labeled: Popular, Hillbilly, and Race.) The most influential trade magazine that charted the records and categorized the listings was *The Billboard*. Basically, the Pop charts were marketed to white urban areas with a catalog of smooth singing crooners, big bands, show tunes, and the like and were almost exclusively white, with some Latin or, occasionally, African Americans such as Nat King Cole, Billy Eckstine, or Ella Fitzgerald. Rhythm & Blues was strictly African American recording artists with a strong lineage of delta blues and a solid downbeat as the forerunner of Rock 'n' Roll. Country & Western (sometimes listed as Folk and in previous years Hillbilly) was marketed mainly to white rural areas of America. The labeling of the music genre within the July 15, 1950 issue of *The Billboard*, for example, listed Hank Williams's records in separate advertisements as Folk, Country, Western, and Country & Western.

Hank Williams (1923–1953) first appeared at the Grand Ole Opry in 1949 when he was 26. Four years later, Williams career was cut short at the age of 30 due to alcohol and drug abuse as he died early in the

morning on New Year's Day in 1953. By the time he first appeared on
the Opry stage, however, he had been playing guitar and singing since
his pre-teens. He was born Hiram King "Hank" Williams in Georgiana,
Alabama. As a teenager he joined a band named the Drifting Cowboys, traveling extensively playing honky-tonks and roadhouses. His
charismatic performance was well received by the Opry audience,
prompting many encores, and helped to propel his career as a Country &
Western singer. During his short, but very memorable career, he wrote
and sang many of his own hit songs including, "Your Cheatin' Heart,"
which was a #1 hit on the country charts; and at the same time on the
top 10 on the pop charts as sung by Tony Bennett. In fact, the legendary
Bennett had his very first hit with another Williams song, "Cold, Cold
Heart." During his short career, Williams charted many hit songs,
almost all of them published by the Roy Acuff and Fred Rose music-
publishing firm, Acuff-Rose ("Hank Williams").

Although his official career lasted just a little over four years, Williams
left a memorable list of hit songs that included, "Hey Good Lookin',"
"I Can't Help It (If I'm Still in Love With You)," "I'm So Lonesome I
Could Cry," "Mind Your Own Business," "Move It On Over," "Honky
Tonk Blues," "Half as Much," "Your Cheatin' Heart," and "Jambalaya,"
to name just a few. His hits often came in "bunches" and were available
for sale and heard on the radio. An advertisement in the July 15, 1950
issue of *The Billboard NAMM Trade Show and Convention Section*, for
example, listed Hank's "Why Don't You Love Me," "Long Gone Lone-
some Blues," and "Lovesick Blues," as the Best Selling Country &
Western Records and also listed them on the top five list of the Most-
Played Juke Box Country & Western Records. That same ad billed
Williams as,

STILL MAKING and BREAKING RECORDS
FEATURED STAR ON WSM GRAND OLE OPRY

Sometimes *The Billboard* listed his songs as "Folk (Country &
Western)." It is unclear why there was an inconsistency, nor why the
need to change the labeling and add the parenthesis (24).

In the years after his death, the Williams legacy was kept alive as
many musical artists from the 1950s through the 21st century recorded
his songs. Some, such as "Hey Good Lookin' " were recorded many
times over by such diverse artists as blues legend Ray Charles in the

1950s, pop crooner Dean Martin in the early 1960s and country group The Mavericks in the 1990s, as well as many others. Another was "Jambalaya," which was recorded and adaptable in different musical styles by the likes of Emmy Lou Harris (Country), Jo-el Sonnier (Cajun), Fats Domino (Rhythm & Blues), Asleep at the Wheel (Western Swing), and literally hundreds of others. Quite a few others also had hit records with Hank's songs including Linda Ronstadt ("I Can't Help It"), LeRoy Parnell ("Take These Chains From My Heart"), Chris LeDoux ("Settin' the Woods on Fire"), Pirates of the Mississippi ("Honky Tonk Blues"), and George Thoroughgood ("Move It On Over), to name a few. During the 1990s, "Move It On Over," was remixed with Hank's original vocals overdubbed in harmony by his son Hank Williams, Jr. and grandson Hank Williams III.

The same July 15, 1950 issue of *The Billboard* that listed some of Hank Williams's songs also listed quite a few other Country & Western

The career of legendary country musician Hank Williams lasted just a little over four years, but he left a memorable list of hit songs that included: "Hey Good Lookin," "I'm So Lonesome I Could Cry," "Mind Your Own Business," "Move It On Over," "Your Cheatin' Heart," and "Jambalaya." This 1951 photo was taken on stage at the Grand Ole Opry. In the background, Chet Atkins is on guitar and Ernie Newton on the stand-up bass. (Courtesy of Photofest.)

singers, including Ernest Tubb and his Texas Troubadours. Tubb was also billed as a Top Selling Folk Artist in Retail Sales and in Jukebox Play. Some of those hit records of 1949 and 1950 included, "Blue Christmas," "Have You Ever Been Lonely," "I'll Love You Because," "I'm Bitin' and Thinking of You" (a duet with the Andrews Sisters), "Let's Say Goodbye Like We Said Hello," and "Slippin' Around" (*Billboard*'s 4th Annual Music-Record Poll, 16).

The Country & Western artists such as Ernest Tubb, Hank Williams, Spade Cooley, Western Caravan, and Bob Wills and The Texas Playboys laid down a tradition that was very well-known in the rural honky-tonks and dance halls, and was gaining some national exposure through Hollywood movies and WSM radio broadcasts of the Grand Ole Opry. However, by the mid-1950s the music was pushed back to regional locales. At the time, a new sound emerged, but that new sound was built strongly upon many of those same Country & Western traditional artists. Western Swing music historian Stephen Thomas Erlewine probably said it best when he wrote, "In time, all of it became raw material for rock and roll" (Erlewine, *All Music Guide*).

Bill Haley, Rock 'n' Roll, and Elvis Presley

During the 1940s and 1950s, Americans settled into a postwar life of prosperity and conformity. Dancing was still a popular trend, and in some cases solely youth-orientated, but refined. Dances for youth were usually formals, proms, cotillions, and sock hops. The cotillion was a formal dance where young debutantes oftentimes still held a dance card and were escorted by hand-picked eligible young men. A sock hop received its name from teenagers who went to a school- or church-sponsored dance held in a gymnasium. In order not to damage the gym floor, teens were asked to remove their shoes and dance in socks. One constant was that all of the dances were usually heavily chaperoned and the dance music was carefully selected. However, by the late 1950s and into the 1960s, a counterculture developed mainly by the emergence of the teenager as a viable demographic within American society. The changing force was driven by Rock 'n' Roll music.

Regardless of the labeling, and also because of the profitability, the quick accession of Rock 'n' Roll ended the nationwide appeal of Country & Western music, pushing the music back to the rural areas. Many of those influenced by Western Swing morphed into the Honky-Tonk sounds of the likes of Ernest Tubb, Webb Pierce, Lefty Frizzell, and Hank Williams. But quite a few, such as Bill Haley and the Comets, were Hillbilly bands that incorporated the Western Swing sound into what some called Rockabilly, but others called Rock 'n' Roll.

Bill Haley (1925–1981) was best remembered for kicking off the Rock 'n' Roll era with his 1954 mega-hit song, "(We're Gonna) Rock Around the Clock." The major impact of Haley and "(We're Gonna) Rock Around the Clock" was that teenagers began dancing as never before. Of the song, music legend Dick Clark stated, "Its initial impact was incredible. Kids hadn't been dancing since the end of the swing era. Suddenly, this spirited tune with a bouncy, rhythmic beat had the kids clapping and dancing." Other rarified Country & Western musical artists that emerged as Rock 'n' Roll pioneers included Buddy Holly, Jerry Lee Lewis, the Everly Brothers, and Elvis Presley (Uslan and Solomon, 17).

Although he was closely associated with the nationwide teenage Rock 'n' Roll craze of the 1950s, Haley was actually a product of the prototypical Western Swing band of his time. In fact, prior to settling on the name of his band as Bill Haley and His Comets, the names of his two previous bands included "Bill Haley and the Four Aces of Western Swing" and "Bill Haley and the Saddlemen." Haley actually started with a Country & Western band, and he soon combined musical styles that at first included country and bluegrass. He also was influenced by the likes of Milton Brown, Bob Wills, and such contemporaries as Spade Cooley. During the late 1940s and into the early 1950s, Haley added the influences of Rhythm and Blues, Jive, and Honky Tonk as he emerged with a sound that was most often described as Rockabilly, or, as some of his contemporaries called his music, "Western Bop." Haley himself once described his musical style as "Western Jive." However, after the release of "Rock Around the Clock" and the application of the term by Cleveland radio disc jockey Alan Freed, Haley's music became universally known as "Rock 'n' Roll."

Beginning in 1951, Alan Freed hosted the late night *Moondog Show* on WJW-AM, a 50,000-watt Cleveland radio station. The songs he played were mainly Rhythm and Blues, and almost exclusively by black artists. The music was often risqué, humorous, playful, and exciting, but most importantly it was defined by a heavy backbeat and was certainly danceable. Freed drew a faithful audience of teenage listeners, both black and white, and termed the music Rock 'n' Roll.

Bill Haley and His Comets were a Hillbilly band that incorporated the Western Swing sound into what some called Rockabilly, but others called Rock 'n' Roll. Haley was best remembered for kicking off the Rock 'n' Roll era with his 1954 mega-hit song "(We're Gonna) Rock Around the Clock." This 1956 photo is from the movie *Don't Knock the Rock*. (Courtesy of Photofest.)

He also sponsored those same artists that he played on the radio at live Rock 'n' Roll shows across America. The first show held in the Cleveland Arena on March 21, 1952 attracted a sold-out crowd of over 10,000 teenagers, both black and white. Many thousands of others were turned away. In 1954, Freed was offered a deal to bring his show to the nation's largest radio market in New York City. Airing a similar format over WINS-AM radio, his popularity soared nationwide—mainly among urban teenagers. At his peak during the late 1950s, he also appeared in Hollywood movies that included *Rock Around the Clock* (1956) and *Don't Knock the Rock* (1956). And a highlight of the movies was not just the music, but also the scenes of teenagers dancing along.

In addition to listening to the music on the radio, teenagers also had access to the new music, although in a much more sanitized from, through television. From 1957, when it went national, until the early 1960s, an astounding 20 million teenage viewers rushed home each day after school to watch the televised late afternoon Rock 'n' Roll music and dancing show hosted by Dick Clark named *American Bandstand*. The national dance show had such a large impact that teenagers all across America had access to the same music and dance styles. But dancing to the same music and doing the same dances did not mean that all teenagers could dance together. At the time, America was still strictly segregated and laws not only prevented interracial dancing, but also prevented integration in most places of public accommodation, especially the dance halls. Dick Clark noted one example in 1959 when he organized a touring version of a Rock 'n' Roll show called the "Caravan of Stars." The nature of a segregated society was apparent as Clark recalled, "In the southeast we had to play before divided audiences—sometimes blacks upstairs and whites downstairs, sometimes split right down the middle with whites on one side and blacks on the other" (Uslan, 61). The municipalities tried to enforce segregation, but the reality was that for the first time both black and white teenagers were sharing the same experiences through a common music.

Teenagers not only listened, they also bought the music as they purchased Rock 'n' Roll records at an astounding rate. In 1950, Americans of all ages purchased 190 million records. By 1960, however, they purchased over 600 million records, of which over 70 percent were purchased by teenagers. The introduction of the Long Playing 33 1/3 (LP) album, 45-rpm record, and portable record players allowed youth the privacy of listening to their preferred music. In 1956 alone, over 10 million portable record players were sold. Many of those portable record players were sold as the result of one artist who during that same year sold almost 4 million recordings alone, and by 1960 had sold 28 million—his name was Elvis Presley (Halberstam, 474).

More than any other artist, Presley defined the image of Rock 'n' Roll. Elvis was a musical pioneer—a young white man whose music crossed the cultural barrier between black and white. According to early blues singer Ruth Brown, "where Elvis was concerned there was no color line, because everybody liked his music." But, Elvis was born poor in rural Tennessee, and grew up with the roots of the music of Blues, Folk, Gospel, and Country & Western. By 1956, Elvis was a nationwide celebrity and the subject of much controversy. One television performance on September 9, 1956 on the *Ed Sullivan Show* (viewed by an estimated 42 million people) showed Elvis only from the waist up. Sullivan thought Presley's gyrations were vulgar and refused to allow his wiggling hips to be broadcast before a national audience. However, Presley was just too much of a nationwide sensation and his popularity soared. He also extended into a succession of profitable Hollywood movies. They were usually light-hearted fun with thin plots but lots of Elvis songs and some dancing. The films included *Loving You* (1957), *Jailhouse Rock* (1957), *Blue Hawaii* (1961), *Fun in Acapulco* (1963), and *Viva Las Vegas* (1964), among others (*Rock 'n' Roll Explodes* 1995).

After Elvis, in 1960, America embraced a new dance craze as Chubby Checker introduced a song and a dance of the same name, "The Twist" on Clark's *American Bandstand*. The simple dance created a sensation as never before seen in American social dancing. Most importantly, it separated the dance partners as they raised up on the balls of their feet and used their arms to perform a "twisting" motion with the body in unison to a Rock 'n' Roll beat. The Twist was an instant sensation and remained the dominant dance craze of the entire century. However, while most of America was twisting the night away, many continued traditional dancing to Country & Western music in rural honky-tonks and dance halls.

The Two Step "Crouch and Gait"

Despite the changing social elements in American entertainment with Rock 'n' Roll dances such as the Stroll, Mambo, and Cha Cha during the 1950s, the Twist and "doing your own thing" in the 1960s, and disco and freestyle dominating the nationwide trends in popular social dancing in the 1970s, many honky-tonks and rural dance halls continued to feature traditional country music. Although not widely publicized, nor for that matter as the result of any nationwide fad, throughout that time many people continued Country & Western dancing in honky-tonks, rural dance halls, community centers, and other similar venues. The favored dances included the Two Step, Schottische, Polka, and the Put-Your-Little-Foot. Western promenade and square dances were also often seen within the dance halls. Occasionally the bands would play old songs of Czech, German, or Bavarian origin.

These were basically the same dances from the Western Swing days of the 1920s and 1930s. Susan Chadwick studied the Two Step in an article for *Texas Monthly*, calling it "a simple step. But done to tricky country rhythm." The style did not change very much as the dancers enjoyed themselves, but there was very little upper body movement or flailing of the arms—nor were there many intricate foot patterns. Chadwick speculated that the pumping of "their arms back and forth in a style" was not evident prior to the 1980s, which coincided with the movie release of *Urban Cowboy* (1980). The basic style, as seen by Chadwick, was "to dance straight ahead, in a great counterclockwise mass." As with all dancing styles, as the Country & Western music changed so did the dancing. One tendency noted by Chadwick was that, unlike pre-World War II days, the couples moved just a little further apart and also "stiffened their legs and arms." Prior to 1980, any type of arm flailing or excessive movement of the arms during a dance "was once considered an embarrassingly hick thing to do." For the most part, Country & Western style of dancing throughout the southwest had a characteristic "crouch and gait" (Chadwick, "The Two Step").

Country & Western dancers in a local honky-tonk. Notice that two different styles are evident as the couple in the center and the couple partially hidden on the left appear to be dancing swing style, and the couple on the far right in a closed dance position indicative of a Fox Trot. (Courtesy Texas Dance Hall Preservation, Inc.)

Many have speculated that the "crouch and gait" style looked like a bowlegged cowboy wearing spurs who had developed the gait from riding a horse. But, scholarly research in Texas determined that the dance style and distinctive posture was derived from actual cowboy gear, but not from riding a horse, but rather from the boot itself. The shape of the sole of the standard cowboy (or cowgirl) boot placed the ball of the foot close to the ground. The sole rose supporting the arch and rose to a heel about one and one-half inches above the floor. Therefore, the rigid contoured shape of the sole resulted in a style that necessitated "dancing on the ball of the foot." Social etiquette also required restrained movements during the dancing of Two Step as the couple glided on the balls of their feet along the floor. The contour of the boot sole also dictated that the individuals have "loose knees," which resulted in a slight bend and therefore a crouch. At the time, the Two Step continued in its basic form and was one of the most common Country & Western dances. Dancing the Two Step was also readily available in many rural and small town honky-tonks and dance halls (Chadwick, "The Two Step").

Honky-Tonks and Dance Halls

In 1957, the Rodair Club opened near Port Arthur in response to the growing teenage demand for Rock 'n' Roll dancing. The dance hall held over 400 people and was quite popular in the immediate area. However, in a reversal of a national trend, after the Rock 'n' Roll fad died down and the Twist and Beatles were the new trend in the 1960s, the Rodair changed its format to Country & Western music and dancing as well as a flavor of Cajun. Both Cajun and Country & Western shared similar dance styles in the Two Step and Waltz. In deference to the national trend, owner Joe Thibodeaux responded, "Cajun music is the best in the world for dancing." As for the devotees who attended he added, "No doubt about it. They come here to dance" (Morthland, "Come Dancing").

Cain's Ballroom and Dance Hall in Tulsa, Oklahoma, that had opened in 1930 continued holding regular Country & Western dances until 1958. Bob Wills and the Texas Playboys had ended their regular engagement in 1943; but Bob's brother Johnnie Lee Wills and his band were hired as replacements, continuing at Cain's until its closure. Throughout the 1930s and 1940s, Cain's often filled to a capacity of

6,000 people. By the 1950s, however, the hall suffered a steep decline in attendance. The decline occurred not only at Cain's, but all across America in dance halls and ballrooms of all dance genres. The main reason was the advent of television that captivated the public and kept people of all ages at home. The decline was evident in all forms of entertainment including dancing, movies, and restaurants, among other venues and activities.

In Texas alone, well over one hundred old-style dance halls offered nightly entertainment and Country & Western dancing. Most of them traced back to the Western Swing days of Bob Wills and Milton Brown, whereas others dated back to the 19th century. Although many in America might have thought that they had just disappeared, the basic fact was that these venues just did not receive much public attention. One common trend was that almost all of them were well removed from urban areas and cities. One prime example was the Tin Hall Dancehall and Saloon located outside of Houston, Texas in the remote area of Cyprus. It dated to 1890 when it was built as a community center. During the emergence of jazz and Western Swing, a second level was added during the 1920s to serve as a dance hall. The large hall often had as many as 2,000 people attending weekly dances. Tin Hall continued hosting weekly dances until it was closed in the 1980s. After a dormant period of a few years it was reopened in response to the *Urban Cowboy* craze.

Farther away from Houston, and some 20 miles north of the Tin Hall Dancehall, was Henry's Hideout. It dated only to 1937, but strictly as a roadside bar. In 1964, as the Beatles were launching the British Invasion and cultural changes upon America, Henry's Hideout added a "back-room dance hall" for Country & Western music and dancing. The total capacity of the bar and dance hall was about 400 people. Another rural dance hall located outside of Longview on Texas Highway 31 in East Texas near the Louisiana border was Reo Palm Isle. Similar to Henry's Hideout, it was also built during the Great Depression in 1935. It was a bit larger with a capacity of 2,500 people and hosted many up and coming country artists, including Elvis Presley. Throughout that time and well into the 1990s, it was open six nights a week "to keep 'em two-stepping" (Morthland, "Come Dancing").

In Fort Worth, the Stagecoach Ballroom with a capacity of 1,000 opened during the pre-World War II heyday of Western Swing. After a fire destroyed the building in 1970, it relocated in Fort Worth and enjoyed a prosperous decade during the 1970s. Nearby, in Dallas, was the Longhorn Ballroom. The Longhorn had actually opened in 1950 under the co-ownership of O. L. Nelms and Bob Wills, and was named the Bob Wills Ranch House. Musician and historian Geronimo Treviño in his study of Texas venues *Dance Halls and Last Calls* (2002) described it as "a traditional honky-tonk with no fancy tablecloths or mirrored balls" (154). Two years later it was sold to Jack Ruby and renamed the Longhorn Ballroom. In November 1963, Ruby became infamous in American history after the assassination of President John F. Kennedy in Dallas. As the supposed assassin Lee Harvey Oswald was escorted out of a prison holding cell, Jack Ruby walked up to him and shot him dead. The event was captured on live television and repeated on the news stations repeatedly, making Ruby a national figure.

Another location in East Dallas was the Debonair Danceland Westernplace, with a capacity of 1,000 that opened during the late 1960s. It maintained an atmosphere of Country & Western music and dancing throughout the 1990s. In 1995, John Morthland in an article for *Texas Monthly* said of the Debonair, "This dance hall has withstood all trends to remain a no-frills urban hall with a pure country house band, called the Original Debonaires." Another Dallas dance hall that maintained the honky-tonk tradition was the Top Rail Ballroom. Also opened during the late 1930s, it was described by Morthland as looking "more like a big honky-tonk than a dance hall." With a capacity of about 600, it was often viewed as "a tough place in a bad area." Others in West Texas included Lubbock's Cotton Club, Amarillo's Aviatrix Ballroom, the Stampede, and the Farmer's Daughter.

The John T. Floore Country Store in Helotes, located nine miles north of San Antonio, Texas, opened in 1942 and was named after the owner. At first, it was actually a combined rural country store with a post office, voting booth, insurance office, real estate office, food service, and a bus stop located directly outside. Soon thereafter, in 1946, an adjoining building was added with a dance hall for 300 people. The dancing proved profitable enough for Floore to close the store and concentrate on the Country & Western music and dancing. Occasionally, when more popular musical acts such as Willie Nelson were booked, an outdoor stage and dance floor was added with a capacity for 1,000 people. Most of the other dance halls had a capacity for around 300 to 750 people. They included the Blumenthal Dance Hall, Club 21,

Coupland Dance Hall and Tavern, Twin Sisters Hall, and Watterson Hall. Gruene Hall, built in 1878, was billed as Texas's oldest continuously running dance hall; a bit older was the Fischer Dance Hall built in 1875, in which parts of a movie starring Willie Nelson in *Honeysuckle Rose* were filmed in 1980. Not too long after, the Fischer Dance Hall closed (Morthland, "Come Dancing," 78–85).

The Swiss Alp Dance Hall in Fayette County was one example typical of almost all the others. German immigrants first built it as a community center and dance hall in 1900. For many years it catered to those favoring Polka style dances. It switched formats during the 1940s, prompted by the popularity of the Western Swing bands. The hall continued with that format through the 1950s and into the 1960s, hosting the likes of Rock 'n' Roll and southern rock bands such as B. J. Thomas and ZZ Top. Swiss Alp Dance Hall closed in the mid-1980s shortly after the decline of the *Urban Cowboy* phase. After a long dormant period, the dance hall was restored and reopened in April 2006 (Corcoran, "Country Dancehalls Preserve Texas History").

Dessau Dance Hall and Saloon (originally Dessau Hall), located north of Austin, was first built as a community center in 1876. Dessau had a diverse dance history as it hosted the big bands of Glenn Miller and Tommy Dorsey, as well as country legends Bob Wills and Hank Williams. In 1968, it suffered a devastating fire, but was quickly rebuilt as a larger dance hall accommodating 750 people. Although nowhere near as old as Dessau, the Broken Spoke in Austin quickly became legendary as a Country & Western dance hall. It opened in 1964, intending "to look like an old vintage dance hall." From the beginning the Broken Spoke started booking Country & Western bands for dancing that included Bob Wills, Willie Nelson, Asleep at the Wheel, George Strait, Ernest Tubb, Hank Thompson, Roy Acuff, and continuing through to the 21st century with the Derailers, Dale Watson, and Jerry Jeff Walker. Some parts of the Willie Nelson movie *Honeysuckle Rose* (1980) were also filmed at the Broken Spoke, as well as *Wild Texas Wind* (1991) with Dolly Parton, a mid-1980s documentary *Dance Across Texas*, and a BBC documentary *Texas Saturday Night* (1991). The Farmer's Daughter in San Antonio opened in 1961 with the same intention as the Broken Spoke. A crowd of about 600 regularly went to hear traditional Country & Western music and, of course, to dance. As with just about every Country & Western dance hall, the crowd did not need any special occasion or prompting to dance. Owner Ivan Romjue

Many of the rural dance halls were simple wooden or metal buildings with tilt up panels at the windows for ventilation during hot summer months. This photo of Kendalia Halle in Texas was one typical example. In 2009, the original wooden dance floor that was installed in 1903 was voted "Best in Texas." (Used by permission of Judith Temple and Kendalia Halle.)

proudly stated, "This is the truest dance crowd: As soon as the band begins to play, the floor fills up" (Morthland, 78–85; Treviño, 71–73).

Most of the dance halls were simple wooden or metal buildings that often doubled as community centers. The simple buildings often had a low-slung hip roof with hinged panels along the wall that were opened and hinged up on hot nights for air circulation such as Kendalia Halle. Although the dance halls and honky-tonks were not nationally famous, they often held special memory for all those that went, especially as children for the first time. Bill Porterfield, for example, recalled that he went to his first honky-tonk named Rob's Place in 1940 at the age of eight. Rob's Place was located in South Robstown, Texas, along U.S. highway 77, about 40 miles west and inland of Corpus Christi, which lay on the Gulf of Mexico. Rob's, as with almost all of the honky-tonks and dance halls, was inexpensive, with limited décor and accessible for all ages. In a recollection of *The Greatest Honky-Tonks in Texas* (1983), Porterfield described Rob's Place as,

A long, low rectangular building, white clapboard. . . . As you entered, the front part of the building had a bar on the right side and on the left, tables and chairs and a couple of pool tables . . . and a shuffleboard. If you were hungry, you could get cold cuts and hot links at the bar, which only served beer and pop. If you wanted to dance, you had to walk through a gate in a little wooden fence that cut off the dance floor from the front. During the day there was no cover and you could dance to the jukebox as long as you had the nickels and quarters. At night if the house band was playing you paid a dollar to get in and had your hand stamped with magic ink so you could come and go without having to pay over again. On special weekends, when a big-name outfit was playing, the cover was doubled and you had to arrive early to get a table around the dance floor. (16)

One of the "big-name" country stars who appeared at Rob's was Ernest Tubb, who was often called the "daddy of honky-tonk music."

Porterfield's familiarity with Tubb's music, and the recordings of other Country & Western singers such as Bob Wills and the Texas Playboys, came from local radio stations KONO from San Antonio and KGKO from Fort Worth. He also remembered hearing them live from the Grand Ole Opry over WSM radio. As a child, Porterfield remembered asking his aunt "if it was disrespectful to get up and dance when a star like Ernest Tubb was singing." His aunt's reply was, "No honey, he wants us to," as she quickly pulled him up and danced while Tubb played one hit song after another (Porterfield, 15). But, neither the simplicity of the honky-tonk, nor the mixed ages of the patrons could suppress the occasional disagreement. On some occasions, a disagreement took place and an occasional fight broke out. During those times, it was best left to the owners to quiet the situation and let the band play on. As Porterfield recalled, "If a fight broke out, the best bet was to keep dancing" (17).

Dancing was the main attraction, especially as a Saturday night activity in just about any of the rural towns. John Morthland described one of the "classic small-town dance halls" as the London Dance Hall, located on U.S. Highway 377 in London, Texas. The dance hall had a capacity of about 800 and drew from the triangular grouping of three towns of Mason, Junction, and Menard; each located about 18 to 20 miles away. It was built just before 1900, with the dance hall added in the 1920s. During the 1930s, it hosted the likes of Adolph Hofner, Jimmie Martin, and the Texas Plow Boys. In an interview with

In this 1944 photo, Ernest Tubb and his band play on stage at the Grand Ole Opry in Nashville Tennessee. In 1940, when Tubb played Rob's Place, a honky-tonk dance hall in South Robstown, one young patron remembered asking his aunt "if it was disrespectful to get up and dance when a star like Ernest Tubb was singing." His aunt's reply was, "No honey, he wants us to." (Photo by Frank Driggs Collection/ Getty Images, Editorial image No. 5091624.)

Geronimo Treviño for *Dance Halls and Last Calls*, Hofner remembered that at London Dance Hall, "Everybody came out to dance, not to sit and listen, and it made you feel good to see them out on the dance floor" (Treviño, back cover).

On one particular Saturday night, John Morthland, who surveyed many of the Texas dance halls in an article for *Texas Monthly*, attended a dance at the London Dance Hall. He described the family-friendly scene,

> Inside, the dance hall was loud, friendly, and animated all at once-the way Saturday night is meant to be. Younger dancers stood in groups, flirting and sizing up their prospects. As the Fredericksburg band Southern Image broke into its countrified version of the Rolling Stones' "Honky Tonk Women," the kids let out a collective whoop. When that ended, the

Cotton-eyed Joe began, and they happily turned the floor over to their parents. The band followed with a medley of Roy Orbison ballads and the kids were back out there dancing real, real close. (Morthland, 78–85)

The dance hall had a reputation for attracting patrons of all ages, as well as family members of all generations. In fact, owner Billy Ivy had family roots in the area dating to the 1850s that predated the formation of London as a town in 1878 along the West Texas cattle trail. Her father, Ty Bo Ivy had assumed ownership and his family regularly attended all the dances. Billy Ivy remembered, "We all learned to dance right here." In summing up the choice of the family gathering in the dance hall on weekends, Ivy added, "Was there ever anything else to do on a Saturday night?" (Treviño, 152–153).

Saturday Night Fever and Disco Dancing

For many, a new Saturday night activity emerged in the form of doing the hustle dance inspired by John Travolta in the movie *Saturday Night Fever*. But, the stage had been set for disco just a decade before. By 1968, American society had changed drastically, mainly due to the antiwar protests of U.S. involvement in Vietnam. At the time, the United States had committed to an all-out war and sent over 543,000 troops to Vietnam. In all, over 58,000 soldiers died in the conflict igniting massive antiwar protests and an upheaval within American society at home. By 1969, antiwar protests and unrest on college campuses extended nationwide. This turbulent period of change in American society was also reflected in its dancing. A generational gap both in society and the dance floor separated Americans. Older adults continued to dance ballroom and traditional Country & Western dances. The younger set twisted off into expressionistic and individual solo dancing. At first a whole slew of non-partner dances came and went. In a short time, these dances did not even have names, nor for that matter did they have any set patterns.

During the 1960s, the freedom of expression on the dance floor coincided with the escalation of the equality movements of all kinds, including gay liberation, Hispanic pride, the American Indian movement, and women's liberation, among many others. The issue of women's equality created heated discussion, mainly by male-dominated conservative and religious organizations. The faction that was strongly opposed to the new sexual freedom allowed by the oral birth control pill was often portrayed as those living in rural areas and also Country & Western singers. Two Country & Western songs of the time that were a direct affront to the counterculture were Merle Haggard's "Okie from Muskogee" and "The Fightin' Side of Me," recorded in 1969. They were actually written to be jokes of sorts, but many conservatives clung to those songs as mocking the hippies and other unruly youth. "Okie," as one example, told of students being peaceful, not partaking in drugs, and being respectful of adults and traditional values. But, in reality, some hardcore country artists such as Johnny Cash, Kris Kristofferson, and Willie Nelson, among many others, thought the opposite. At the time, Loretta Lynn's song "The Pill" supported women's equality, but many Country & Western radio stations across America refused to play the song, due to its reference to the birth control pill. On the other hand, Tammy Wynette sang of another growing reality spelled out in the title of one of her hit country songs, "D-I-V-O-R-C-E."

Nevertheless, many in the mainstream media portrayed Country & Western music in the image of anti-Hippies. Some critics even charged that the new sexual freedoms and dancing were the result of being in a drug stupor; others blamed the nonconformist Hippie movement. As a result, a strong conservative opposition to the hippies and the freestyle expression in social dancing arose. The opposition viewed the nonconformist counterculture and drug use as a threat to traditional American values. In turn, a "Generation Gap" was proclaimed that posed a social class distinction between those over the age of 30 and those under 30. That distinction was mainly an alterative lifestyle for youth that included freedom of sexual expression, rock music, and political protests. Drug use and flamboyant lifestyles were also controversial when disco emerged.

A 1975 song, "The Hustle" by Van McCoy, set a resounding constant danceable beat, which gave rise to the dance of the same name. The song quickly sold over 10 million copies and kicked off the national disco craze. On one end, the Hustle dance returned to partner dancing, incorporating turns and moves reminiscent of the swing era. In 1977, the disco dance fever hit nationwide on a scale never before imagined with the release of the movie *Saturday Night Fever* starring John Travolta. The next year the disco soundtrack to the movie sold an unprecedented 25 million copies (more than three times the previous leader) and remained at #1 on the album charts for 24 consecutive weeks. In a short

By the mid-1970s, a generational gap both in society and the dance floor separated Americans. Those under 30 were drawn to the flamboyant disco dance style and others danced freestyle expression to both rock and disco music. Older adults continued to dance ballroom and traditional Country & Western dances. In this 1978 photo, an older couple in New Iberia, Louisiana, dance to Country & Western music at the Blue Moon. (Photo by Philip Gould/Corbis PG006286.)

time, disco music of all kinds sold at a rapid rate. Some seemed surprised, but as Dick Clark explained, "disco is just music with a very heavy beat. It's not listening music; it's dancing music." And dance is what Americans did, at over 10,000 venues featuring disco music and dancing in all areas all across America (Uslan, 349, 425).

3

Urban Cowboy
and the Two Step

"An urban cowboy doesn't have to know how to brand or rope or hog-tie or bulldog . . . but he does have to know how to dance."
—Aaron Latham, *Esquire* 1978

By 1980, the memory of the turbulent times of the Vietnam War had faded from the American consciousness. For the most part, so did the freewheeling urban lifestyle of the late 1960s and 1970s typified by the Hippie counterculture and the flamboyance of disco. After a decade notable for gas shortages and long lines of automobiles at the gasoline pumps, Americans entered into the 1980s with a promise of abundance. The call for social change returning to conservative middle-class values was implemented with the inauguration of Ronald Reagan as the 40th president of the United States in January of 1981. Reagan also promised a stronger U.S. presence as a world power and revived Cold War tensions. He escalated the nuclear arms race with the Soviet Union, spending billions of dollars on a missile and defense system program known as "Star Wars." Reagan often echoed the image of the cowboy and the old West, often sporting a cowboy hat himself. The image was often replicated in television shows such as the top-rated *Dallas*, a program about a Texas oil family, and movies such as *Urban Cowboy*. Combined with the movie trend there was a nationwide rise in country dancing and western wear, as many sought once-again to emulate John Travolta. However, this time it was not disco dancing but Country & Western dancing; and the Brooklyn nightclub 2001 Odyssey was now Gilley's—a cavernous Texas dance hall.

The End of Disco and the Beginning of Country

Almost as suddenly as the 1970s came to an end, so did the Disco era. At about the same time, without missing a beat Country & Western music and dancing spread nationwide. To some the change might have appeared drastic; however, there were some striking similarities. Dance historian Ian Driver, in *A Century of Dance*, noted the influence of the disco era upon Country & Western dancing. He wrote,

> One lasting effect of disco was the 1970s and 1980s renaissance in country and western and line dancing. Although the two dance cultures were different in style, disco had inspired a resurgence in the popularity of both couple dancing and line dancing, and as disco's star was waning, a victim of its own success, country music was on the rise. (216)

By that time, although the genesis of Country & Western dancing could be traced all the way back to the early settlers across the North American continent, it was not until the 1980s that Country & Western dancing spread across all areas of America.

In many American cities and towns, the 20,000-plus former discos replaced their glitter format with Country & Western music, dancing, and décor. For a short time, around 1979 and 1980, some hybrids of "Country Discos" fared well. The idea, as Peter Applebome of *The New York Times* noted, was the spread of a new fad. He wrote, "In an age when every fad sprouts another, country disco is the hottest new entertainment in the Southwest." Other hybrid country discos, with simple names such as Cowboy in Houston, and Disco in the smaller Texas city of Strawn, attracted young clientele offering the flashing lights and thunderous non-stop DJ-mixed country and disco music conducive for freestyle dancing. Applebome termed it a "blend of disco technology and urban cowboy chic." More often than not, the dancing was done to contemporary country music artists such as Eddie Rabbitt, Willie Nelson, and Hank Williams, Jr.

Many of those same establishments were returning to their roots of country music that they had only recently moved away from due to the overwhelming popularity of disco music and dancing. Many of those establishments were located in areas well removed from the major urban cities. But in a short time, Country & Western music and dancing also took hold in nontraditional "country" cities such as New York, Chicago, and Los Angeles. The trend quickly spread from coast to coast to all sorts of towns and cities.

Urban Cowboy and "The World's Largest Honky Tonk"

Similar to *Saturday Night Fever*, which seemingly set off an overnight national sensation in disco dancing, another movie, coincidentally also starring John Travolta, did the same for Country & Western dancing, music, and clothing. In 1980, the movie *Urban Cowboy* also created an incredible nationwide surge of interest in everything country and western. In turn, a whole slew of Americans also traded in their three-piece white disco suits for denim jeans, cowboy hats, and boots, while heading to similar establishments in their towns and took a Two Step twirl around the dance floor. For the most part, almost as soon as the Travolta-led disco dance craze had first swept into Houston in early 1978, the movie *Urban Cowboy* was in production in Pasadena a few miles outside of Houston. The filming took place in and around the Texas outskirts of Pasadena, but mostly within an actual Honky-tonk named Gilley's.

Much like the 2001 Odyssey dance club in *Saturday Night Fever*, prior to the filming of *Urban Cowboy*, Gilley's was also a well-established music and dance hall. One journalist from the *Austin Chronicle* said that even before the movie, Gilley's had the "reputation as the mother of all Texas honky-tonks." Susan Orlean in her book *Saturday Night*, proclaimed,

> Some people date the beginning of great Saturday nights in Houston to 1971, with the founding of Mickey Gilley's, one of the original, archetypal citified-cowpoke bars, where . . . new Houston—could dress up in ten-gallon Stetson [hats] and two hundred dollars Tony Lamas [cowboy boots] and drink toasts to a Wild West they never knew. (177–178)

The original Gilley's did open in 1971. At the time, Sherwood Cryer owned and operated a smaller saloon named Shelly's located at 4500 Spencer Highway in Pasadena, Texas. Cryer was known for booking hard-core, up-and-coming country acts, including Hank Williams Jr.

and Willie Nelson. With the attraction of country acts such as Williams and Nelson, Shelly's often filled to its capacity of 500. After a few years, however, Cryer thought that a regular country house band would be better. He remembered seeing Mickey Gilley and the Bayou City Beats perform at the Nesadel Club only about a mile away on the same Spencer Highway. The two agreed for Mickey Gilley to play six-nights a week and, with an offer of co-ownership, changed the name of the venue to "Gilley's" (Gray, "The Mother of All Texas Honky-Tonks").

At about that same time during the early 1970s, the Houston and Beaumont areas of Texas were booming due to an abundance of natural oil deposits. In turn, workers were needed in the petroleum fields and on the oil rigs, thereby creating an influx of migrant workers not only from Texas, but also from nearby Oklahoma and Louisiana. In areas outside of Houston such as Pasadena, the migrant workers congregated and lived mainly in trailer parks. An article in the *Austin Chronicle* described Pasadena, Texas, as "a blue-collar patchwork of strip malls, subdivisions, refineries, and pipeline immediately southeast of Houston." Those migrant workers, who were mostly fans of Country & Western music, also sought the regular entertainment offered by the likes of honky-tonks such as Gilley's.

In a short time, many "urban cowboys" such as Dew Westbrook frequented Gilley's almost every night of the week. Since they worked the oil fields and not the ranches or rodeo circuit, Dew and the others were often classified as "urban" or "drugstore" cowboys. In the country world, only those that actually rode horses or roped steers considered themselves real cowboys. For the most part, prior to the use of "urban cowboy" the term most often applied for a wannabe horseless cowboy was "shitkicker." With the nationwide popularity of country dancing the term, was often softened to "slick kicker." At Gilley's, however, the regulars were known simply as "Gilleyrats." According to Christopher Gray of the *Austin Chronicle*, the Gilleyrats "showed up every night to drink, dance, fight, flirt, make out, bullshit, shoot pool, and see who got their nuts cracked on El Toro, the club's famed mechanical bull" ("The Mother of All Texas Honky-Tonks").

With the increased demand, co-owners Sherwood Cryer and Mickey Gilley enlarged the former Shelly's, added air-conditioning, and rigorously advertised the revamped honky-tonk. The club had a mechanical bull, pool tables, a shooting gallery, punching bags, numerous bar areas, and "a dance floor big enough for thousands." It stayed open seven days a week from 10:00 in the morning to 2:00 a.m. Combining all this with the music of Mickey Gilley and the Bayou City Beats as a "hot house band," people poured into Gilley's night after night—oftentimes there were close to 6,000 people on any given evening. To top it off, the *Guinness Book of World Records* listed Gilley's as "World's Largest Honky Tonk" (Milligan, "Gilley's").

Gilley, a consummate entertainer often described with "a Panhandle-wide grin and a repertoire spanning fiery, piano-pounding rockabilly and shimmering pop standards" also tirelessly promoted the club. He secured a weekly television show on a local Houston channel, and also purchased many radio ad spots on a 50,000-watt Houston country radio station, KIKK. The radio station, prominent in and around eastern Texas, promoted its call letters both over the airwaves and with thousands of bumper stickers as "Proud to be a KIKKer." By that time, according to journalist Bob Claypool of the *Houston Post*, who in 1980 wrote a book *Saturday Night at Gilley's* about the club, said, "Gilley's was, quite simply, the most *Texan* of them all, the biggest, brawlingest, loudest, dancingest, craziest joint of its kind ever" (9).

Besides the promo spots, KIKK radio also played Gilley's songs. In 1974, Mickey Gilley scored the first of many top-10 radio hits with "Room Full of Roses." The song was first played over KIKK radio and was soon a nationwide #1 hit on the country music charts. Many other song hits followed, including, "I Overlooked an Orchid," "Window Up Above," and "Don't the Girls All Get Prettier at Closing Time." In 1976, "Don't the Girls" was voted as the Country Music Association (CMA) Song of the Year. Gilley's quick success led to a nationwide tour, which meant he could no longer play regularly at his own club. Nevertheless, his recording and touring allowed him to promote his club, thereby garnering more attention and eventually the filming of the movie *Urban Cowboy* (Gray, "The Mother of All Texas Honky-Tonks").

In 1980, only a few years removed from the disco dance floor in *Saturday Night Fever*, John Travolta once again turned to the hardwood dance floor and kicked off another nationwide dance craze with the movie *Urban Cowboy.* Travolta's new movie also had some similarities with his disco-era classic. Both movies, for instance, were inspired by national magazine articles. *Saturday Night Fever* was based on a June 1976 *New York Magazine* cover story titled, "Tribal Rites of the New Saturday Night," by Nik Cohn. Although Cohn's story combined many real-life individuals into one fictionalized central character named Vincent, it was centered (and eventually filmed) in a real-life Brooklyn disco dance club named "2001 Odyssey." Vincent was a working class Italian American who by day worked a dead-end job in a hardware store, but on Saturday night released it all by dancing. As a result of the dancing, Vincent was a "somebody," as all those in the club "cleared a space for him . . . right at the very center of the dance floor." Cohn's story became the basis for the hit movie *Saturday Night Fever* (Cohn, 31).

Unlike the fictional character of the disco-dancing Vincent in "Tribal Rites of the New Saturday Night," the characters in an *Esquire* article on Saturday night urban cowboys were real-life. The subject of an "Urban Cowboy" first appeared as a September 12, 1978, cover story in an *Esquire* magazine article written by Aaron Latham, titled: "The Ballad of the Urban Cowboy and America's Search for True Grit." (*True Grit* was a 1972 Hollywood western starring John Wayne, who subsequently won a Oscar for Best Actor.) At the time, disco was also riding high, and the subtitle on the cover proclaimed "Saturday Night Fever Country and Western Style." In early 1978, Latham, a former Texan transplanted to New York to work as a columnist for *Esquire*, contacted Gilley's co-owner Sherwood Cryer about writing a story on life within the Texas honky-tonk.

Rather than center the story on co-owner and music star Mickey Gilley, Latham observed the crowd and got to know the regulars. In fact, Cryer later reported that Latham was fully engrossed in the environment and enjoyed the "drinkin' beer and dancin' " (Claypool, 99). Latham chose instead to highlight two of the Gilley's regulars named Dew Westbrook and ex-wife Betty. Latham described the Westbrooks' life as similar to a stereotypical country song, inserting the "twang" which was a common knock by non-country music aficionados against a supposedly sameness of sound. He wrote,

> Dew met Betty at Gilley's, *twang-twang*. Dew fell in love with Betty at Gilley's, *twang-twang*. They had their wedding reception at Gilley's, *twang-twang*. But they quarreled over the bull at Gilley's, *twang-twang*. And then Dew met somebody new at Gilley's, *twang-twang*. (22)

Similar to those who criticized the sameness of the disco sound, some criticized Country & Western music with a stereotypical sameness of the music characterized by a "twang" or "twangy sound." A popular running joke at the time was, "What happens when you play a Country & Western song backwards?" The answer, "Your dog comes back to life, you find your pick-up truck, and your wife comes back to you."

In fact, Dew had first met Betty by simply asking her to dance—a custom described by Latham as, "An urban cowboy doesn't have to know how to brand or rope or hog-tie or bulldog . . . but he does have to know how to dance" (24). But, soon thereafter, Dew met another women at Gilley's, also by asking her to dance. Eventually, Dew and Betty divorced, and as the story continued in real life, Dew and his new girlfriend Jan continued to go to Gilley's, as did his ex-wife Betty. Each continued not only to dance, but also to ride the soon-to-be famous mechanical bull. Co-owner Sherwood Cryer remembered that during his research Latham "even rode The Bull once" (Claypool, 99).

Both of Travolta's movies had similarities, as each portrayed a dark side of the reality of escaping to the dance halls. In a review in *The New York Times* in June 1980, movie critic Vincent Canby, called *Urban Cowboy*,

> The most entertaining, most perceptive commercial American movie of the year to date. Here is a tough-talking, softhearted romantic melodrama that sees a world that is far more bleak than the movie, or the characters in it, ever have time to acknowledge. . . . [*Urban Cowboy*] is mostly about what he and his friends do at the end of the day, dressing up in their spotlessly clean cowboy gear and setting off to Gilley's to drink, fight, make sexual connections (some more intense than others) and prove their manhood by getting onto a mechanical bull for $5 a ride. (C21)

But real-life issues aside, when the story was made into the movie, it was Travolta's dancing that made the lasting impression.

Arguably, when *Urban Cowboy* was released, Travolta's mechanical bull riding also spurred a nationwide craze; but it was his dancing that eventually proved more popular. Prior to Travolta taking even one step on the dance floor, however, he was criticized by the real-life Dew Westbrook. When he first met Travolta during the initial filming at Gilley's, the real-life Dew said, "John, I don't mean to hurt your feelings or anything, but there's no way you can play me—you're just not country enough, you're disco!" Travolta's simple answer was, "But of course I can play you, I'm an actor." But, Travolta was more than an actor, he was an accomplished dancer adept at incorporating a natural

John Travolta dancing in a scene from the movie *Urban Cowboy* (1980). The movie was filmed in the original Gilley's Club in Pasadena, Texas. (Courtesy of Photofest.)

real-life style into his onscreen dancing. In fact, Travolta proved so adept at learning the Country & Western dance styles that many thought he had been doing the Two Step and the other country dances for many years. To prepare for the movie, choreographer Patsy Swayze coached Travolta. (She was the mother of actor/dancer Patrick Swayze, best known for his role as Johnny Castle in the 1987 movie *Dirty Dancing*.) Under the tutelage of Swayze, Travolta practiced the mainstay dances including the Two Step, One-Step, Three-Step, Texas Polka, the Schottische, and the Cotton-Eyed Joe (Claypool, 109).

The Movie Premier and El Toro—The Mechanical Bull

In June 1980, *Urban Cowboy* premiered in Houston with two big parties. One was an "invitation only" party for over 1,800 "Houston socialites." Each of them paid $125 to hob-knob and rub shoulders with John Travolta and the other stars of the movie. At the same time, another party was held about 30 miles away from the "socialite" party at Gilley's for over 3,500. Within a few days the movie opened nationwide and was an instant success. Soon thereafter, newspapers all across the country carried stories of the new "Urban Cowboy" mania. At first, many of the stories told of the mechanical bull known as "El Toro." In October 1980, *The Associated Press*, for example, announced "Bucking bull mania spreads; Thousands pay to get thrown." AP reporter Mark Schwed described the bull, "It bucks. It spins with a frightening fury, enough to challenge accomplished rodeo riders and scare the daylights out of bar hoppers from New York to Japan. But they love it and the fad is spreading" ("Houston Celebrates Urban Cowboy").

The bull was so popular that those establishments that had similar mechanical devices were in demand. In Nashville, Tennessee, both Cactus Jack's and the Blazing Saddles Saloon reported lines out the door and stretching down the block waiting for an attempt to ride the bull. Others, such as a former Florida disco named Nichol's Alley in Gainesville, changed its format to country and its name to Lone Star and also purchased a mechanical bull. Attracting mostly college students, Lone Star was often filled to capacity at 1,300, and many regularly rode the bull. When they were done with the bull, they often two-stepped to Country & Western music. Although participation was popular, many others simply went to watch the dancing and the bull. The entertainment value of the mechanical bull offered an opportunity to stand by and watch as riders were thrown off.

Getting thrown off the mechanical bull, however, was almost always at the mercy of the operator. The operation included both the speed and bucking mechanism that was controlled by a sideline operator. According to AP reporter Mark Schwed, the manipulation of the control by a "twist of a finger can make the difference between an exciting ride and a sore neck." He described one incident,

> The pretty, blue-eyed blonde dusts off her Calvin Klein's and hops on the mighty 800-pound bull. A man behind the bar pulls a switch. The monster comes to life. The crowd cheers, but only briefly. In seconds, the girl is lying on her backside, another victim of "El Toro."

The mania spread all over America, as all sorts of bars and saloons installed similar mechanical bulls and thousands of people from all walks of life rode the bull nightly.

Urban Cowboy not only sparked a nationwide desire to Two Step: it also spurred a nationwide craze in mechanical bull riding. The mania spread all over America as all sorts of bars and saloons installed similar mechanical bulls, and thousands of people from all walks of life rode the bull nightly. In this December 1980 photo a patron rides El Toro at the original Gilley's Club in Pasadena, Texas. (Associated Press 801217028.)

The mechanical bull, designed by Joe Turner of Mexico, was originally conceived as an efficient training device for rodeo riders. Turner was not quite sure how one of his bulls ended up at Gilley's in Pasadena, Texas, as a nighttime attraction, nor why it was so popular. Nevertheless, the bull was in great demand, and he eventually built and sold over 600 mechanical bulls. However, his health prevented him from continuing, and he soon sold the production rights to Mickey Gilley and Sherwood Cryer. The co-owners of Gilley's were soon swamped with orders from nightclubs in cities and towns not only all over America, but also the world. The demand increased the price of each mechanical bull from $2,100 to $7,995, but the orders continued. Jerry Willrich, who managed the mechanical bull divison known as Gilley's Bronco

Shop Inc, confirmed the deluge of orders and the problem of filling all the orders. Willrich explained, "We just can't make enough of them, even with a day and night shift and an expanded factory." He added, "We shipped out 181 yesterday and have about 120 back orders. . . . We're getting orders from Sweden, Australia, Belgium, Japan, South America and Mexico." In a short time, for the most part, many found that the mechanical bulls were just too dangerous, and for others the fad simply wore off. Dancing on the other hand, was not only safer, but also proved to last longer (Schwed, "Bucking Bull Mania Spreads").

The Travolta Two Step

Similar to *Saturday Night Fever*, the most lasting impression from *Urban Cowboy* was Travolta's dancing. In particular, according to *New York Times* movie critic Vincent Canby, "There is also dancing in 'Urban Cowboy,' mostly the Texas two-step" (C21). But at the time that Travolta was adapting to a new dance style, disco was sweeping the nation. During the filming of *Urban Cowboy*, the Bee Gees were also touring on the success of their *Saturday Night Fever* soundtrack album and the disco fervor sweeping the nation. At one concert at the Summit Arena in Houston, coincidentally on a Saturday night, Travolta made a surprise guest appearance at the Bee Gees concert. As the group launched into the song "You Should Be Dancing," Travolta appeared on stage and in front of over 18,000 fans performed his solo disco dance from *Saturday Night Fever*. Although he was sporting his "country beard" and still best known as a disco dancer, in a short time, Travolta's dancing in *Urban Cowboy* inspired many Americans to undertake a new Saturday night activity: the Texas Two Step.

The Two Step is the most well-known of all the Country & Western dances, but it is also a bit of a misnomer. It was often danced in different tempos and rhythms and also had slightly different variations. It was also a bit different than the late 19th century American dance also known as the Two-step. Actually, the older 1890s traditional dance was more like the triple step pattern of the 1980s Western Polka. The late 20th century Two Step was a basic walking step rhythm of quick-quick, slow-slow. (The "quick" is one beat of music, whereas the "slow" is two beats of music.) Unlike the similar rhythm of the Fox Trot which can be either progressive line-of-dance or in a box step, the Two Step is always danced in a progressive counterclockwise motion along the perimeter of the dance floor known as the "line-of-dance." Similar to the Fox Trot, sometimes the Two Step is also danced in a rhythm of slow-slow, quick-quick. In either case, the line-of-dance was always strictly maintained and the idea was to continually keep moving. In theory, any couples dancing in time with the same rhythm of the music would all be moving progressively at the same speed; but in reality that was not always the situation. Oftentimes, a slower couple would need to let a faster couple move past them. Most often, the slower couple would dance closer to the inside perimeter while the faster couples moved along the outside.

In *Kicker Dancin' Texas Style*, authors Shirley Rusher and Patrick McMillan observed that the slower Western Two-Step was more popular when live bands played and the faster Texas Two Step was more often danced while a DJ spun a record. Rusher and McMillan likened it to the "tempo and rhythm pattern" of the pre-1920 Fox Trot. However, the Texas Two Step was simply described as "the western version of the Ballroom Fox Trot." When the tempo moved faster to western swing, the dancers often incorporated breakaway movements and whips and turns from the Jitterbug and Lindy Hop and the dance was sometimes termed the Houston Whip. In turn, the country version, while danced in the traditional line-of-dance, was known as Texas Two Step Swing. Depending on the different regions in America, the same dance rhythm might often be called by a different name, including the Slow Two-Step, Walking Two-Step, Cowboy Two-Step, Shuffle Two-Step, or Kicker Two-Step, among others (74).

The basic handhold was the standard ballroom closed position with some regional variations. In the version that Travolta danced in *Urban Cowboy*, he placed his right forearm on Sissy's (actress Debra Winger) left shoulder with his palm turned downward firmly placed behind her shoulder blade. His left hand grasped her right wrist and held in to the side and below waist level. Sissy draped her left arm low and hooked her finger onto his belt loop. This basic "cowboy hold" allowed the man to lead the lady by gently pushing her in line-of-dance with his right arm while his left hand allowed for some basic turns. Travolta moved forward and Winger, following, went backwards as they performed the foot pattern in unison. In *Urban Cowboy*, they danced a Texas Two Step version with a rhythm of side-together-side—step. The "side-together-side" moved them slightly out of the line-of-dance as the "step" came after a brief pause at the end of the basic, and brought them back into the line-of-dance. Travolta also emulated the reality of the standard posture of the Two Step and the cowboy hold with a slight "hunch" as he moved around the dance floor. Movie choreographer Patsy Swayze commented on how Travolta quickly adapted not only to the dances, but also captured the natural styling. Swayze noted, "When he does the waltz, he's so erect and princely. And when he does the two-step, he can bend down and get that cowboy hunch" (Claypool, 116–118).

In later years, as the Two Step spread nationwide, many did not adapt the natural styling of the hunch, but rather chose the basic ballroom hold. As a result, the Two Step did not necessarily resemble the indigenous honky-tonk style, but appeared more stylized similar to Ballroom competition. In addition, the basic Two Step that was most commonly taught throughout the United States did not have the partners go into the side-together-side diagonal motion, but rather stayed within the formal line-of-dance. At the time, just as Travolta and Winger danced in the movie, most two steppers stayed in the basic dance frame without breaking the dance hold. In later years, partners added numerous underarm turns, whips, tunnels, and other intricate moves, as well as other dance styles such as Polkas, the Waltz, and western swing, among others.

Western Swing, Polka, Triple Step, and Put Your Little Foot

Western swing was often danced line-of-dance to faster rhythms, combining many more turns and gyrations while continually moving progressively forward in the line-of-dance. In later years, couples moved into the center of the dance floor or on the corners, and danced western swing as a spot dance more resembling the 1930s jitterbug. By the 1990s, western swing was standardized as two spot dance variations known as East Coast Swing and West Coast Swing.

The Western Polka was basically the same as the traditional 19th century Polka that was introduced to America by way of Paris and traced back to a 1830s Bohemian folk dance. During the mid-1890s, as the Polka maintained a sense of refinement in eastern American ballrooms, it was also brought westward with the settlers and cowboys, who often incorporated exaggerated hops and lively movements. In many instances, the Western Polka was quite similar to the traditional

Of all the dances in Country & Western, the most well known is the Two Step. In this photo the man leads forward and the lady follows backward in progressive line-of-dance. From *Kicker Dancin' Texas Style* by Shirley Rushing and Patrick McMillan, p. 97, © 1988. (By permission of Hunter Textbooks.)

Polish Polka as danced throughout the United States during the same time. Oftentimes it was called the Texas Polka or simply the Triple Step (Rusher and McMillan, 274).

Similarly, the Ten-Step Polka as danced during the 1980s (and also sometimes called the Heel and Toe Polka) was a predetermined 10-step derivative of the 19th century Polka variations. The Western Waltz was also basically the same as the traditional dance in 3/4 time dating back to the Volta of the Middle Ages. Shirley Rusher and Patrick McMillan in *Kicker Dancin' Texas Style* noted the 19th century Waltz as danced in the eastern urban ballrooms migrated "westward with the American cowboy and . . . continued to grow in popularity" (177).

Comparable to the Waltz, the Varsovienne was danced in 3/4 time and was first popular in America during the mid-1850s. In *The Round Dance Book*, Lloyd Shaw said the Varsovienne was "one of the loveliest and one of the best-loved of all the old-time dances" (245). At the time, the Varsovienne was sweeping the eastern ballrooms it was also danced extensively in Spanish California and throughout the Southwest among Mexican Americans who called it "La Varsouvianna." During the late 19th century in Texas, it was danced by both those of Mexican ancestry as well as arriving immigrants and settlers, and was often referred to as the "Little Foot" dance. The Varsovienne was danced in many, if not all, of the Texas dance halls from the mid-1850s through the 1980s. During the 1980s, Put Your Little Foot, a popular "Kicker Dance," was basically the same as the 19th century Varsovienne. The basic "cross, step, point" of the 1850s Varsovienne pattern also remained quite similar to the 1980s "cross, step close" of the Put Your Little Foot (Giordano 2006, 177–178).

The Cotton-Eyed Joe: "What Chu Say?"

By the 1980s, of all the dances, the crowd favorite was certainly the Cotton-Eyed Joe. Unlike the partner dances, the Cotton-Eyed Joe is a spoke-wheel line dance with as many as six to eight persons standing side-to-side with linked arms lined up behind similar rows of linked-arm enthusiastic dancers. They performed simple polka-type steps around the perimeter of the dance floor. The dance is the ultimate in enthusiasm, as the dancers often whoop and holler and sometimes respond with loud shouting in unison when prodded by the band. One uninitiated observer simply described it as they "stomp around the floor yelling barnyard expletives." Newspaper journalist Christopher Gray of the *Austin Chronicle* was a bit more direct and also more accurate. Gray's first-hand observation noted that Americans on "dance floors coast to coast resounded with cries of 'Bull-shit!' as non-Texans from Tucson to Toledo lined up to learn the two-step and Cotton-Eyed Joe" ("The Mother of All Texas Honky-Tonks").

For the most part, the Cotton-Eyed Joe is an adapted polka step in a spoke-wheel formation of which the basic elements were also evident in some traditional square dance formations. In *Kicker Dancin' Texas*

Style, Rusher and McMillan described the Cotton-Eyed Joe as "an authentic slavery song . . . [derived] from an Irish folk song." They claimed the original song combined Irish clogging steps with African footwork danced to an old Irish melody (22). Yet, despite the similarities, it is considered to be an original Texas dance. Some sources indicate that it might have developed as the distinct spoke-line round dance in response to a Bob Wills's western swing adaptation of the song "Cotton-Eyed Joe." During the 1930s when Wills played the song, the dancers almost instinctively lined up in a spoke-wheel square dance formation. In turn, they started with a heel-toe step, followed by a backward shuffle. The basic simple step was very similar to the 19th century dance the Heel-toe Polka (Casey, 17).

In 1967, musician Al Dean recorded a lively instrumental version of "Cotton-Eyed Joe" that proved quite popular among dancers in rural honky-tonks. Dean recalled that it was about the same time that dancers, in direct response to his version, replaced the traditional "heel-toe" with the swing kick of the leg. Similarly, in response to the lively tune, they added all sorts of whoops and hollers, but all in good fun. Soon thereafter, the Cotton-Eyed Joe was a standard among the honky-tonks and Country & Western dance crowds for years. In fact, it was a rowdy crowd favorite that was often danced while dancers firmly clenched a longneck bottle of beer; having one or even both of their arms around the waist of an adjoining dance partner. In 1980, Bob Claypool in *Saturday Night at Gilley's* called it, "The finest most distinctive line dance of the contemporary Texas shitkicker." He had witnessed the dance almost every night at Gilley's and described it as,

> Hundreds of cowboys and cowgirls are packed onto the Gilley's dance floor, lined up side-by-side, arms around each other's shoulders or waists, all facing in the same direction. And when those lines move, chugging and stepping in counter-clockwise revolutions around the floor, they look like the spokes of a wheel, with the very center of the floor serving as a hub. (Claypool, 168)

Much of the popularity of the Cotton-Eyed Joe could be attributed to the rambunctious impromptu of just about any kind of shouting, whooping, or hollering throughout the dance. Some would even create various cadences reminiscent of a square dance caller prompting a response from the all too eager dancing crowd. Either the DJ, the band, or even the dancers themselves would shout out a call. The most popular prompt to ask the crowd was, "What do you say?" which, more often than not, came out with a slight slang and was heard as "What 'chu say?" In unison the response from the dancing crowd was usually, "Bullshit!" Betty Casey in *Dance Across Texas*, might have humorlessly claimed that the application of the word "bullshit" with the dance motion of the swinging leg was matched with a familiar barnyard occurrence. It was common when working on a farm while attending to the barnyard animals to occasionally step in animal droppings. Therefore, Casey said that the swinging leg motion was similar to "the act of kicking off barnyard muck" (17). Nevertheless, the basic dance was described as follows,

---

COTTON-EYED JOE

DESCRIPTION: 24-count, PROGRESSIVE LINE of DANCE

MUSIC: *Cotton-Eyed Joe* (traditional) by many artists;
Cotton-Eyed Joe by Rednex

BEAT/STEP DESCRIPTION:

SWING KICK, BACKWARD SHUFFLE

1 – 2	Swing Left Leg Out and Over Right, Kick Left Leg Forward.
3 & 4	Triple Step Backwards, Left Foot, Right Foot, Left Foot
5 – 6	Swing Right Leg Out and Over Left, Kick Right Leg Forward.
7 & 8	Triple Step Backwards, Right Foot, Left Foot, Right Foot.
9 – 10	Swing Left Leg Out and Over Right, Kick left Leg Forward.
11 & 12	Triple Step Backwards, Left Foot, Right Foot, Left Foot
13 – 14	Swing Right Leg Out and Over Left, Kick Right Leg Forward.
15 & 16	Triple Step Backwards, Right Foot, Left Foot, Right Foot.

SHUFFLE FORWARD

17 & 18	Shuffle Forward, Left-Right-Left
19 & 20	Shuffle Forward, Right-Left-Right
21 & 22	Shuffle Forward, Left-Right-Left
23 & 24	Shuffle Forward, Right-Left-Right

BEGIN AGAIN

These dance instruction sheets, similar to the one for the Cotton-Eyed Joe, as they existed were not always grammatically correct. Typically a good caller asked a question on the swing kicks and the response came as the dancers shuffled backward. Many of the shouts were often applied to common everyday occurrences to which the dancers could relate. At Gilley's, one typical cadence prompted by a lively fiddle player went as follows:

Caller: "Stepped in what?"	Response: "Bullshit!"
Caller: "Smelled like what?"	Response: "Bullshit!"
Caller: "What chu say?"	Response: "Bullshit!"
Caller: "The job'll get easier?"	Response: "Bullshit!"
Caller: "Gas'll get cheaper?"	Response: "Bullshit!"
Caller: "What chu say?"	Response: "Bullshit!"
Caller: "Say You Just Got Rich?"	Response: "Bullshit!"
Caller: "Can't Quite Hear Ya?"	Response: "Bullshit!"

For some, the improvisation lasted through the whole dance with a new set of questions for the four series of swing kicks and backward shuffle steps. The response was always the same—"Bullshit!" (Claypool, 168–169).

During the mid-1990s, a European group named Rednex recorded an electronic dance mix version of "Cotton-Eyed Joe." At the time, prior to its release in America it was the largest selling single throughout the world. In fact, it was one of the largest selling singles in the history of recorded music. The popular catchy tune was soon in demand in the country dance clubs. However, the song was so popular that wedding DJs picked it up, and children at grammar schools also loved the song. Needless to say, at family functions, and especially with children present, the "Bullshit" response was usually omitted.

Dancing Styles at Gilley's

Country dancing, as did just about every other form of American social dancing, served either one or another purpose. One was simply to dance for fun and relaxation. The dancing could be alone, with a partner, or even with a variety of partners. The other reason for dancing was as a means for finding a sexual partner. In either case, the relaxed

1. Closed position, waist-hand (ballroom) hold

2. Semiclosed position, waist-hand (ballroom) hold

3. Open position, shoulder (varsouviana) hold

4. Drill-line, rock position, no hold

5. Facing position, handclasp hold

6. Circle position, handclasp hold

7. Spoke-line position, waist hold

Some of the different Country & Western dance positions. From top left: 1. The closed position was most often seen in the Two Step, Triple Step, and Waltz. 2. Semi-closed for swing dances. 3. Open Position for Put Your Little Foot and perimeter couple dances. 4. Drill-line for line dances. 5. Face to face position for West Coast Swing and others. 6. Circle for square dancing. 7. The Spoke line position for the Cotton-Eyed Joe is at the bottom right. From *Dance Across Texas* by Betty Casey, Copyright © 1985. (By permission of the University of Texas Press.)

atmosphere of Country & Western dancing allowed for either one or the other, or sometimes both. Barry Durand a dance teacher and owner of a country dance nightclub named the Country Junction in Rockville, Maryland, remarked, "For singles and couples alike, it's a great way to meet people in a comfortable way." A main reason for the comfortable atmosphere was the ease of the Country & Western dance style. As Durand often explained to his students, "There are no wrong moves in country dancing. . . . If you miss a step, so what? Someone will lead you or teach you the correct step" (Crowley, "Ballroom Dancing, Cowboy-Style," 14).

Shortly after the movie journalist and music critic Bob Claypool chronicled the real life Gilleyrats in *Saturday Night at Gilley's*, he noted that local regulars such as Gator Conley prescribed to "The Code" of the dance floor. Conley, due to his dancing ability, was one of the featured dancers in *Urban Cowboy*. Many of the Gilley's other regulars were also hired as movie extras. Eventually, the film crew employed over 800 extras, many of them either Gilley's regulars or local Pasadena residents. As for Conley's dancing, Claypool described it as follows,

> Whether alone with his partner on the vast floor or packed in tight on a hoorawin' Saturday night, Gator remained true to his beliefs and each movement was executed with maximum grace and precision—done *right*! . . . Gator usually chose his partners for their corresponding skill on the floor, not for their availability. (Claypool, 90)

As for using dancing as a way for finding a sexual partner, Conley claimed that "using the dance floor for such a thing seemed wasteful and wrong." Although he admitted he "chased woman," he preferred other junctions within the club rather than the dance floor (Claypool, 90–91, 125).

Conley was born in Louisiana and transplanted by his parents to Houston as a youngster. However, he did not grow up exposed to dancing. In fact, during his first marriage both he and his wife went "honky-tonkin" but, they did not dance. In one Houston honky-tonk named Wahoo Lounge just off the Gulf Freeway, he came across an older gentleman named Lloyd Reily. Gator remembered, "boy, could he dance! He was the smoothest thing you ever saw." Encouraged by Reily and edged on by his wife, Conley soon learned to dance.

He remembered, "I started to learn how to dance like that, and I picked it up pretty fast. . . . I patterned myself after Lloyd Reily and I still have his style" (Claypool, 92).

Soon thereafter, in 1972, he went to Gilley's to see Willie Nelson and Mickey Gilley. According to Conley, although Nelson went on to major musical success, many of the Gilley's crowd said "they couldn't dance to Willie's music." Undeterred, Conley became a Gilleyrat and by 1975, after he split-up with his wife, he had by his own admission "acquired an extreme desire for dancing" (Claypool, 93).

At the time, during the early 1970s, many people still equated any dancing done to Country & Western music as square dancing. As the Two Step and other similar dances spread nationwide and received media attention, some of the misnomers were eliminated. Newspaper columnist Pat McNees of *The Washington Post,* as one example, noted, "Most people think country dancing is square dancing. It's not. It's a cowboy version of ballroom dancing—but more laid back and energetic, and with more of a sense of forward motion" (McNees, "Let's Shuffle, Pardner," N6).

At the time the media attention also listed the available places for Country & Western dancing along with addresses, telephone numbers, and names of local dance instructors. McNees, for example, noted that in the greater Washington, D.C., and northern Virginia area there were many opportunities. Groups formed such as the Northern Virginia Country Western Dance Association (NVCWDA) and organized events such as weekly or bimonthly dances. These groups also organized dance weekends at Buffalo Gap, and a dance camp in Capon Bridge, West Virginia. Numerous others sponsored Country & Western dances such as on alternate Fridays and Saturdays at venues such as Elks Lodges, fire department halls, and roller rinks. Most relied on a DJ playing the music and a dance instructor to teach lessons. McNees also noted in *The Washington Post* article that almost all of the Country & Western dances were places "where even a city slicker or single woman can feel comfortable trying out the two-step" (McNees, "Let's Shuffle, Pardner").

Another local example was Country Junction in Rockville Pike, Maryland, located at the rear of the Colonial Manor Inn lobby. Latela's in Jessup, Maryland, on Route 175 off the Baltimore/Washington Parkway offered live music Wednesday through Saturday. McNees called it a "friendly, popular country & western dance club, with the biggest dance floor of all the nightclubs." Raffles 2 at 620 Lakeforest Boulevard in Gaithersburg, Maryland, had "only a small dance floor" and limited Country & Western dancing to only Sundays, but, according to McNees, it was noted for attracting "some really good C&W [country & western] dancers." The Village Barn at 6601 Suitland Road, Morningside, located one-half mile from Andrews Air Force Base, sponsored basic Country & Western dance classes on Tuesdays and live country bands on alternate weekends.

In Virginia, the "rustic, down home" Partners 2 at 13401 Lee Highway on Route 29 held Country & Western Thursdays on a decent sized dance floor. Zed at 5151 Richmond Highway in Alexandria advertised live Country & Western music every night. The small dance floor, however, was not totally conducive for dancing, nor for the new-to-country crowd. McNees noted, "The crowd and atmosphere vary considerably and this is not always a comfortable place for single women. I was told some bands attract a crowd that might feel rough to city slickers" (McNees, "Let's Shuffle, Pardner").

Country Dancing Spreads Nationwide

The Cotton-Eyed Joe and the movie *Urban Cowboy* certainly struck a chord with Americans' fascination with Country & Western dancing. Gilley's prospered tremendously from the movie as thousands flocked to the club. In keeping with the mega size of the Texas honky-tonk, co-owners Cryer and Gilley added on a 10,000-seat rodeo arena and also a radio and recording studio for a nationally syndicated *Live at Gilley's* radio program on the Westwood One network. Many of the programs were also released as LPs. Actually, from 1977 to 1989, almost all of the live country acts were recorded, some for LP release, and all for broadcast weekly over KIKK and a network of 500-plus radio stations as "Live from Gilley's." Tied in with it all was also a merchandizing campaign including T-shirts, belt buckles, and even beer cans by the Spoetzl Brewery adorned with the image of Mickey Gilley. The self-promotion of Gilley's was further enhanced as the logo appeared onscreen in *Urban Cowboy* at least 100 times. The logo was behind the stage, behind the bars, and even emblazoned on the ceiling tiles (Gray, "The Mother of All Texas Honky-Tonks").

In an attempt to capitalize on the mania, many other "country-styled" music and dance halls opened in areas all across the nation. In San Francisco, for example, over 125 opened, most catering to dancing. San Francisco actually had a "hotline" telephone number for "prospective two-steppers" to locate a Country & Western dance club. For that matter, so did many others all across America. Likewise, 15 similar type dance saloons opened in Denver; and another 30 or so opened in Boston. Closer to the source of inspiration, Houston which had about 10 or 12 honky-tonks before the movie, numbered almost 300 after the movie. Actually, while *Urban Cowboy* was still in production, clubs in and around Houston rapidly changed formats from disco to Country & Western. One Houston-based conglomerate launched a nationwide chain of 40 dance clubs combining both country and disco music. Some of the more successful included Fool's Gold and San Antone Rose, both located in affluent neighborhoods. And, unlike the working class clientele of Gilley's, they catered to the likes of, as one journalist called them, "Gucci gauchos." Staying closer to the roots of true honky-tonks, another Texas entrepreneur from Fort Worth opened a "super-saloon" billed as the "world's largest nightclub." The three-acre honky-tonk called Billy Bob's had over 40 bar areas dispersed on four levels as well as two 7,000-square foot dance floors. To go one better than the standard mechanical bull, Billy Bob's had an indoor rodeo area with 10 live bulls (Demarest, "C & W Nightclubs: Riding High").

Prior to *Urban Cowboy*, many of the dance halls and honky-tonks had a long-established tradition, while others sensing a new trend opened Country & Western themed restaurants and bars. Fueled by the success of *Urban Cowboy*, quite a few also provided dance floors. Some, such as Cowboy's in Fairfield County, Connecticut, catered to a specific clientele. John Brejot, a DJ on WKHK one of New York City's country music stations and music programmer at Cowboy's, observed that local business people often traveled and spoke of Country & Western establishments they had visited in other parts of the country. Often, according to Brejot, the experience was described as they "had the time of their lives." Therefore, he saw an opportunity and provided a country themed bar "aimed at an upwardly mobile group." Cowboy's, and others like it, provided a "slick" atmosphere styled more towards restaurant fare. With the nationwide fad created by *Urban Cowboy*, many others copied similar formats, many aimed at creating a Country & Western themed atmosphere. As Joel R. Weber of *The New York Times* noted, " 'Practically every slick country bar that's opened in the two and a half years since has been a spin-off or a copy" ("Disco Yields to Western Swing," 13).

That same desire also carried over into country music, especially in areas not known for the genre. During the mid-1970s as disco ruled the airwaves, a little over 600 radio stations featured all-Country music formats. By the beginning of the 1980s, over 2,000 radio stations all across America switched to all-Country music formats. One prime example was in New York City, with two radio stations, WHN-AM and WKHK-FM, reaching hundreds of thousands of country music fans in and around the tri-state area of New York, New Jersey, and Connecticut. WHN at 1050 on the AM dial had switched formats in New York to all-Country as early as 1974. By 1976, WHN was rated the number two radio station in what one critic noted as "the most discerning radio market" in America. Shortly thereafter, WKHK at 106.7 FM advertised "Country Music in Stereo." The FM station engineered a marketing blitz promoting, "New York is Putting Its Boots On." Advertisements appearing in magazines and subway stations showed the Statue of Liberty donning a pair of cowboy boots. WHN also instituted a similar high-powered ad campaign on New York City buses and trains featuring pop country crossover artists such as Linda Ronstadt, Kenny Rogers, Dolly Parton, Emmy Lou Harris, Crystal Gayle, Anne Murray, and the one and only Elvis Presley. At the time, spokespeople from both stations claimed that the shift to country music was more than just a fad (Livingston, 60–61).

Within the range of both WHN and WKHK was Fairfield, Connecticut. But, according to Fred H. Roos, unbeknownst to many, "country music has always had a following in Fairfield." Roos, who held a day job in a lamp factory, was lead singer in a local Country & Western band named Middle of the Road. Dressed in faded jeans and sporting a gray beard, Roos was described by journalist Joel Weber of *The New York Times* as, "Connecticut's answer to Willie Nelson." The band often had a full schedule in and around the local area in places such as the White Birch Tavern in Newtown, the Entertainers Lounge in Norwalk, the Old Gate Saloon in Milford, the Hayloft in New Milford, or the Whiskey River Saloon in New Haven. All located in Connecticut, they booked not only local bands such as Middle of the Road, they also booked bands from Tennessee, Texas, North Carolina, and Arizona.

During the early 1980s, over 2,000 radio stations all across America featured all-Country music formats. One prime example was in New York City, as WKHK-FM at 106.7 FM engineered a marketing blitz promoting "New York is Putting Its Boots On." This mid-1980s advertisement that appeared in newspapers, magazines, and subway stations showed the Statue of Liberty donning a pair of cowboy boots. (Author's Archives.)

The main appeal was traditional Country & Western music for dancing. Unlike the cavernous dance halls such as Gilley's and Billy Bob's, the Connecticut dance floors were quite small. Despite the restrictions, dancing to Country & Western music was the main focus ("Disco Yields to Western Swing," 13).

In 1981, Weber on assignment for *The New York Times*, surveyed the nationwide trend in the changeover from disco to Country & Western. In an article, "Disco Yields to Western Swing," he reported that music and dance clubs sported a new look. He wrote, "Out are spike heels, white three-piece suits and heavy makeup. In are silver belt buckles, alligator boots and feathered cowboy hats." The names of the clubs from Hartford, Connecticut, to Dallas, Texas, and Los Angeles, California, also alluded to the country theme. They included such names as, Charlie Horse, Chaps, Outlaws, Lone Star Cafe, San Antone Rose, Silver Saddle, Gopher Gulch, and Wild Wild West, among many other similar types of names. One former Chicago disco dance club named Outlaws that had featured—of all things—"mud-wrestling disco," quickly switched to the Country music format. In keeping with the "western" theme, Outlaws even included a mock shooting game complete with western-style six-shooters. Just to be safe, the guns were loaded with blanks. Despite the approach for interactive authenticity, most of the clubs just featured live country music ranging from local bands to top name artists ("Disco Yields to Western Swing," 13).

Journalist Michael Demarest of *Time* concurred with Weber's ad hoc 1981 *New York Times* survey. Demarest, on the other hand, termed the new Country & Western styled clubs "sagebrush saloons . . . [with] lively rustic dancing." In addition to the obvious differences in décor and music, however, Demarest noted a striking similarity to disco— mainly the profitability of the new trend. He added,

> Only a year ago, many of the new spots were disco clubs, whose stylized allure has faded fast in some locales. Now decked out with steer horns, long bars, and waitresses in Stetsons and hot jeans, they have struck a bonanza. ("C & W Nightclubs: Riding High")

Typical of the trend noted by Weber and Demarest, one former disco in Dallas named "The Pawnshop" located on Greenville Avenue, a busy entertainment strip in Dallas, changed its format and name. Diamond Jim's eliminated its sleek disco décor and in its place installed wooden barstools, lots of saddles, spurs, and an occasional mounted deer head. Other examples that did the same opened in Dallas, Houston, St. Louis, Memphis, and New York. Rick Archer, a local Houston instructor and disco dancer, noticed the quick change-over. He recalled, "In the spring of 1979, by my count, over a dozen Disco clubs switched to Country in the span of just four months." One of those was the former disco, "Mirage," which revamped its décor and changed its name to "San Antone Rose." Likewise, other discos including the Rubaiyat, Foxhunter, and Xanadu seemingly overnight became Bullwhip, Cowboy, and Desperado ("The Arrival of 'Urban Cowboy' ").

For one club in New York City, the trend actually began a few years earlier with the opening of the Lone Star Cafe in 1977. Although the Lone Star Cafe remained opened well into the 21st century, it did so by catering more to the longneck bottle beer-drinking crowd rather than dancing. The Northeast was often perceived as a nontraditional country area, but it often surprised some country aficionados. Houston natives Deborah and Gregory Hines, who had relocated to Fairfield, Connecticut, were unaware that the New England area knew both the music and dancing. Granted in colonial times through the early 19th century English Country dancing was firmly entrenched as an American tradition in that same area, but Country & Western dancing just did not have roots in New England. But, when City Limits opened in 1981 in nearby Norwalk, Connecticut, Deborah Hines said, "We were surprised to see that anyone up here could do what we thought were regional dances." City Limits, as one example, provided the total atmosphere of an escape into the Country & Western world of the music, dancing, and fantasy. Carl Pandell, co-owner of City Limits, explained,

> We're working hard to fill our dance floor with the best country dancers in southern New England. . . . We try to provide a wholesome environment, where people can drink, dance and have fun. . . . Plenty of folks around here just want to be a cowboy for a night. We let them.

The dancing at City Limits included the Two-step, Cotton-Eyed Joe, Western swing, Polkas, the Shuffle, and a few line dances (Applebome, "Country Meets Disco," C1).

As part of his survey, *Time* journalist Michael Demarest visited City Limits. Unlike the fast-paced flamboyant disco club atmosphere, the changeover to country music also applied the laid-back atmosphere associated with the rural west. Demarest observed,

> Indeed most of the country-and-western clubs aim for an image of laid-back conviviality, rather than the high-strung competitiveness of the discos they are replacing. The beat is slower, the music more sentimental, and touch dancing is back. Couples on the floor whirl through the Texas two-step, cotton-eyed Joe's, heel-toe polka, and country swing—even

waltzes and foxtrots. A number of clubs offer nouveau westerners free
dance lessons—though, as one owner puts it, "the steps are easy to fake."

But, City Limits was just one of many new country-style dance clubs
that did not rely on the fact that the patrons knew the dances; instead
they offered dance lessons. The dancing was not limited to just weekends. On one particular Monday evening at City Limits, over 80 people
showed up early to take advantage of the free country dance lessons.
Nearby to City Limits, and also in Norwalk, another venue named
Appaloosa followed the same trend. However, they went one step
further. In addition to the dancing, they even offered patrons an opportunity to ride a mechanical bull just as John Travolta had done in the
movie *Urban Cowboy* (Demarest, "C & W Nightclubs: Riding High").

Kicker Dancing and Line Dancing

The nationwide desire for all things country was centered on the desire
to dance. But, as one Houston area dance teacher Rick Archer noted,

> Before *Urban Cowboy* very few people danced Western here in Houston.
> For one thing, there was zero demand for Western dance classes. Indeed
> I had never received even one request to learn how to Western dance. For
> example, in 1977 and 1978, I had not had one person ask me to teach
> Western lessons.

In fact, prior to the movie, individuals learned to country dance either
from family or by frequenting a honky-tonk. But soon thereafter, dance
instructors all over America, including Archer, had full classes ("The
Arrival of 'Urban Cowboy' ").

Archer was a self-described "former disco dancer" who got the bug
for Country & Western dancing. Initially, he, as with so many others,
was a bit bored by the simplicity of the Two Step, Triple Step, and
other similar dances. However, after the movie *Urban Cowboy*, many
former disco dancers such as Archer gravitated towards the Country &
Western dance floors, and they started incorporating turns and spins
from the Hustle dance with the standard Two Step, Polka, and country
Waltz. Prior to the time when disco converged with Country & Western
dancing, most of the Two-stepping stayed in the closed position. In
contrast, disco and the Hustle involved many stylized moves and turns
alternating with both the open and closed position. However, simply

applying them to the Two Step was not easy. Archer remarked, "Every night out on the floor I could see dozens of couples experimenting with awkward one-hand turns and clumsy side-by-side cuddle moves ala Disco." This problem at first was attributed to the fact that the Hustle was a spot dance and the Two Step was a progressive line-of-dance, or as Archer proclaimed, "This was Disco on the Run!" Some of the Country & Western dancers did a moving Two Step that incorporated spins and turns reminiscent of the Lindy Hop and was known as the Houston Whip. A good example of the contemporary Houston Whip was evident in the movie *Urban Cowboy*. In a short time, however, the disco moves were figured out and soon thereafter, the Two Step and the other mainstays of Country & Western dancing became more stylized (Archer, "Disco Rises from the Ashes").

The overwhelming desire for Country & Western dancing also prompted numerous "how-to-dance" books. Fresh on the heels of the *Urban Cowboy* movie, Tony Leisner authored *The Official Guide to Country Dance Steps* in 1980. Leisner's book basically featured the dances done in the movie. In fact, he noted that the dancing was simply called "Kicker Dancing" in Texas. He offered photographs with two Gilley's regulars, Gator Conley and Peggy Wright, demonstrating the basic couple dance positions and line dance positions. For the partner dancing, Leisner offered four basic "rules" for the dance floor as follows,

- The man usually dances forward.
- The woman usually dances backward.
- Couples usually dance counterclockwise around the outside of the floor.
- Beginners and those doing less straight-ahead routines should use the center of the floor to avoid collisions with those on the outside.

Of all the dances, Leisner called the Texas Two Step "the simplest dance to learn." His "official" Gilley's version included a repeated pattern of three steps, which was a rhythm of quick-quick, slow, and quick-quick slow in either 2/4 or 4/4 time. He also diagramed partner dances for the Polka (called "Pasadena Polka"), Waltz, and Schottische. Beside the partner dances, he also described the basic line dance positions. They included the spoke wheel for the Cotton-Eyed Joe; the "straightforward stance," which was side-by-side facing forward similar to military drill line; the single file, in which dancers stood facing the back of the person in front of them; and the Bunny Hop position, lined up single file placing hands on the hips of the person in front, similar to the 1950s Bunny Hop and 1930s Conga line (Leisner 1980, 66–70, 78).

By the time *Urban Cowboy* was released, line dancing was routinely done in the Country & Western dance halls, although nowhere near the complexity or overwhelming popularity as during the 1990s. Unlike partner dancing such as the Two Step and spoke wheel types such as the Cotton-Eyed Joe, line dancing did not require a specific partner. The dancers lined up in rows with equal spacing between them and performed set choreographed dance steps in segments matched to the various 16-, 24-, 32-, and 64-count phrasing of a particular song. (Later line dances had other combinations.) Prompted by a caller (usually a DJ or band member) the entire group started with the same foot and moved in unison (hopefully) all in the same direction. Upon completing the sequence the entire group turned in unison and repeated the sequence again facing a different location in the dance club. Most of the contemporary line dances contained basic vine steps and heel out together steps with an occasional simple one-quarter turn to both end and begin a repeated sequence. Some contemporary line dances included the Cowboy Boogie, Flying Eights, and Slapping Leather, to name but a very few. At the same time, one country song, "Elvira," by the Oak Ridge Boys, did have a line dance of the same name choreographed for the song.

Line dancing such as the Bus Stop featured in *Saturday Night Fever* was quite prominent within the disco dancing era. Although line dancing had earlier precedents in the 1950s with the Madison and the Stroll; as well as the Shim Sham in the 1930s, they were not as numerous as during the 1970s. By the mid-1970s, line dancing was common in the disco dance clubs, featuring the Bus Stop, L. A. Hustle, the Walk, the Rollercoaster, the Hollywood Line Hustle, and the Hot Chocolate, among many others. In 1978, dance instructor Karen Lustgarten in *The Complete Guide to Disco Dancing* claimed that the Bus Stop (sometimes known as the L. A. Hustle) was "the line dance that launched a thousand others" (86). Actually, Jan Brackenbury's Country & Western description of the Bus Stop in her 1986 publication *Kountry Kickers: Country Western Line Dance Manual* was slightly different than Lustgarten's. Brackenbury described it as follows,

Do a 3 step grapevine, kick left foot. Do a 3 step left grapevine, kick right foot. Staring with right foot, take 3 steps back and kick with left foot.

Rock forward on left foot, rock back on right, rock forward on left. (Put weight [on] left foot) and kick right foot while turning 1/4 turn to the left. Start dance over. (Brackenbury, 55)

Brackenbury's Country & Western description might have been slightly different than Lustgarten's disco description, but hers was actually the same as the Electric Slide, which was a contemporary non-country line dance of the time.

In 1985, Betty Casey in *Dance Across Texas* observed that some contemporary line dances associated with Country music had just crossed over from "rock music." The Tush Push, was a prime example. As one of the most notable of all the country line dances, the Tush Push was originally choreographed around 1980 for "rock music" and not for country music. The "Four Corners," was another example, described by Casey as a "no-hold, drill line dance that crossed over into the Texas country-dance category in the 1980s." She also noted another early line dance in a military drill line was a simply an adaptation of the 1960s Hully Gully. The development of the contemporary line dances was mostly an outgrowth of the new Country & Western themed establishments. Most replicated the music and dancing, but not necessarily all the features of the old honky-tonks (20).

In 1984, the Hollywood movie *Footloose* portrayed the struggle of a "hip" Chicago teenager named Ren McCormack (actor Kevin Bacon) who moved to a small fictional midwestern town named Bomont. Within the town itself, Ren found that, as a result of the persistent preaching from the local reverend, the town's residents were convinced that all dancing was a sin and therefore prohibited. The story continued as Ren hoped to persuade the town council and the reverend to rescind the ban and allow dancing at the high school prom. Despite it all, the town council held firm and rejected his appeal. Although the kids eventually promoted their own dance right outside the town limits, the dancing was less a part of the movie than the struggle for the right to dance. During the course of his acclimation, and his overwhelming desire to dance, Ren was coaxed by some of his fellow students to cross the county line. The group went to a local honky-tonk and Ren lost no time in dancing Country & Western. In the scene from the movie, Ren and girlfriend Ariel (Lori Singer) danced a combination of some freestyle and kicker dancing. Along with friends Willard (Chris Penn) and Rusty (Sarah Jessica Parker) the group continued dancing, however, in a scene right out of a real-life ornery honky-tonk Rusty danced with another cowboy prompting Willard's jealousy and a fight. The movie was a surprise hit, mainly because of the dancing.

Texas Dance Halls

Although many of the new dance clubs modeled themselves on the ideal of Gilley's and *Urban Cowboy*, most recognized that Gilley's was a bit more ornery in real life than actually portrayed in the movie. One former "Gilleyrat" recalled, "If they don't get into at least one scrap, they think their weekend is wasted." On the other hand, for many traditionalists *Urban Cowboy* represented a move toward the pop sounds and away from the roots of Country music. According to Geronimo Treviño III in *Dance Halls and Last Calls: A History of Texas Country Music*, the Urban Cowboy fascination "was a movement that took part of the roots away from country music" (46). Despite, the nationwide trend, many honky-tonks remained wedded to traditional country music and dancing. In Texas, for example, dance halls numbering well over 100 and off the beaten path did not follow the nationwide trend. Those same dance halls offered nightly entertainment, usually a jukebox during the week and live bands on the weekends. Many of the halls served double duty as a recreation hall, community center, or opportunity for a catered celebration. Gail Folkins, a self-described "dance hall wife" and author of *Texas Dance Halls: A Two-Step Circuit*, observed "the [dance] halls as meeting places were filled with energy" (xiii). The energy was usually displayed on the dance floor. The aged wooden floor boards, usually over a crawl space, often creaked as dancers two-stepped across the floors of the old dance halls.

The names of the old dance halls varied from those named after ethnic roots and local towns. They included the German Dance Hall, Swiss Alp Dance Hall, Twin Sisters Hall, Gruene Hall, Roundup Hall, Sanger Halle Dance Hall, Luckenbach Dance Hall, and Anhalt Dance Hall, among many others. Many dated from the first homesteaders to the Southwest during the 1880s. During the late 19th century, the area was settled mostly by German, Czech, and Scandinavian immigrants, who in turn built many of the rural community and cultural centers that also served as dance halls. Folkins noted that they served as "an important link in the transmission of ethnic culture from one generation to the next" (Folkins, xiv). By the mid-1900s, the individual ethnic cultures melded into a unique Texan culture all its own influenced by Mexican, Spanish, Creole, German, Bavarian, Polish, and Czech. Most, if not all, relied on live bands, and in the rural Texas dance halls' success was measured not in applause, but by how many of the patrons were up and dancing. Shortly after *Urban Cowboy*, a British BBC documentary called *Texas Saturday Night* chronicled the century old dance halls.

Club 21, named due to its location on Highway 21 in Uhland, Texas, dated to 1893 with an expansion for a dance hall in 1912. For good measure, a small bowling alley for Ninepins was added during the early 1930s. In contrast, the Broken Spoke in Austin, Texas was built in 1964 with the intention of appearing as if it had been built a century earlier. It proudly displayed a sign at the front entry that read, "Through This Door Pass the Best Country Music Dancers *in the* World." Anhalt was another example that was over 100 years old. It was first built in 1875 and later expanded in 1908, with a bandstand added a short time later. Geronimo Treviño observed that by the 21st century, Anhalt was still open and displayed a sign over the front entry, "Anhalt 1908." In keeping with Anhalt's dance floor etiquette one sign read, "No Shorts-Pedal Pushers-T-Shirts or Blue Jeans Allowed on the Dance Floor. Indecent Uncommonly Dancing in This Hall Is Strictly Prohibited." Actually, according to Treviño, it was not until the early 1980s that hats and jeans were allowed to be worn inside Anhalt Hall. Prior to that time, it was basically the unwritten rule in many of the dance halls. The trendy idea of wearing a cowboy hat indoors and on the dance floor was another outgrowth of the *Urban Cowboy* fad (Treviño, 53–55, 71–72, 94).

Cowboy Fashion and Designer Jeans

Another offshoot of the nationwide *Urban Cowboy* trend was fashion. In large numbers, Americans donned jeans and cowboy hats, headed to country-themed establishments in their towns, and took a Two Step twirl around the dance floor. In a similar manner, many did not even dance or frequent a honky-tonk, but still wore cowboy attire. Television shows such as *Dallas* swept in on the wave, and the show's fictional character J. R. Ewing (actor Larry Hagman) sported a cowboy hat,

Line dancing from the Broadway stage version of *Urban Cowboy*. Evident is the distinct line dancing posture and "cowboy fashion." (Used by Permission of Paul Bartz, Windwood Productions and Aaron Latham.)

as did newly elected president Ronald Reagan. By 1982, cowboy fashion, or "Texas Chic," was all the rage. As William K. Stevens of *The New York Times* noted in April 1982, "Cowboy dress, cowboy music and cowboy dancing became the rage from New York to Los Angeles." For the most part, those who simply enjoyed dancing traded in their disco sequin and polyester attire for jeans, hats, and boots. America embraced the cowboy image well beyond the dancing. Dungarees were now called "jeans," and when designed by the likes of Christian Dior, Calvin Klein, Gloria Vanderbilt, and Jordache, they became fashionable "designer jeans." The designers did not stop at the pants, as they also fashioned hats, shirts, belts, and boots. Needless to say, all of the fashion designer cowboy clothes were also quite expensive (Stevens, "Cowboy Culture Yields," A16).

Popular features on all "jeans" were embroidered back patch pockets, typically on one pocket on the right butt cheek, with all sorts of embroidery, ranging from advertisements for Gilley's and Lone Star beer to the names of country artists or the brand name of the jeans. Shirts also displayed all sorts of embroidery. Some purchased authentic western wear in department stores, while others used mail-order catalog companies such as Shepler's located in Denver, Colorado. Within the first year of the changeover, Shepler's, one of the largest western wear stores in America, reported a 75 percent increase in sales. In addition, many boot manufacturers reported that they were unable to keep up with the demand for cowboy boots (Demarest, "C & W Nightclubs: Riding High").

Carolyn Hughes Crowley, on assignment for the *Christian Science Monitor*, observed the fashion in Country & Western clubs in and around the Boston area. She described the simple and comfortable styles,

> Country dancers wear jeans, mid-calf, free-flowing skirts, and flats or heeled shoes. The real devotees spin and twirl in costumes with fringe, beads, bangles, scarves, and exotic-skinned cowboy boots and beaver felt hats costing $60 to $4,000—some with gold inlay and feathers. ("Ballroom Dancing, Cowboy-Style," 14)

Pat McNees of *The Washington Post* observed similar trends in northern Virginia. McNees described it as, "Dress is casual, and cowboy boots are common. . . . Some women wear jeans, but many wear dresses or skirts" ("Let's Shuffle, Pardner," N6).

Then again, the trend among working cowboys remained basic Wranglers and Levis. In turn, many other urban cowboys patterned themselves in similar fashion. Age-old companies such as the founder of denim jeans Levi Strauss & Co. simply known as "Levi's," and Wranglers experienced an upswing in sales. The comfortable fashion certainly transmitted over to the dance floor. One Virginia truck driver explained his preference for country western style over ballroom was mainly due to the clothing. He said, "country is livelier, and I prefer wearing cowboy boots and a cowboy hat rather than a tuxedo" (Crowley, "Ballroom Dancing, Cowboy-Style," 14).

Gilley's Ends and the Legend Lives On

Unlike the traditional honky-tonk where drinking was the major reason why people went in the first place, the 1980s dance explosion proved just the opposite. For the most part, many of the new converts to the Country & Western scene were attracted because of the dancing and not the drinking. In a survey of Country & Western establishments for *The Washington Post* in and around the Washington, D.C., and the northern Virginia area, columnist Pat McNees observed the trend. As one example, McNees noted that the new converts were certainly excited about the dancing, but on the other hand noted, "They're also not here to drink, except for the odd beer or two." In response to the decline in revenue, one waitress explained, "The problem is, country dancers, like ballroom dancers—and unlike disco dancers—don't drink, so they can't give a bar the support it needs." Overall, the amount of Country & Western aficionados declined by the end of the 1980s. The lack of alcohol sales most likely contributed to the decline, but also for many the fad simply wore off (McNees, "Let's Shuffle, Pardner," N6).

By the end of the decade, the heyday of Gilley's also came to an end, although, it was not due either to a decline in beer drinking nor the desire to dance. The end of Gilley's was mainly due to some disagreements between the co-owners Mickey Gilley and Sherwood Cryer. Money was the issue, as property taxes mounted and went unpaid. Gilley claimed that profits from the honky-tonk were mutually agreed to be split evenly, but that Cryer had shortchanged him. A bitter court case followed, with Gilley awarded, by some accounts, in the area of $14 to $17 million in back revenue. Gilley's officially closed in 1989, and in July 1990 the vacant building suffered a devastating fire.

At about the same time that Gilley's closed, America was faced with a drastic drop in oil prices. As a result, thousands of oil field workers lost their jobs. Times of economic recession usually meant that honky-tonks were the place to ease the pain. In and around the Houston area that meant when someone either was either laid off or wanted to blow off steam they went to Gilley's to get drunk, ride the mechanical bull, punch the bag, or dance. However, as Christopher Gray of the *Austin Chronicle* observed, "Maybe that helped ease the sting when thousands were laid off after the price of oil crashed." But, the downturn was a bit too long and the economy did not fully recover in time for Gilley's to feel the effects (Gray, "The Mother of All Texas Honky-Tonks").

However, the legend of the name lived on as Mickey Gilley also secured the rights to use his name on another club that he opened, Gilley's Dallas, and later on, Gilley's Las Vegas. In turn, the promotional items continued, both with the new venues and in outlets such as the QVC home shopping television network. In 1999, a QVC marketing division, Q Records released a long series of *Live at Gilley's* recording artists. Some of the musical acts were all recorded live from the sound-board while the original Gilley's was still open, and included Carl Perkins, Fats Domino, Jerry Lee Lewis, Johnny Paycheck, the Bellamy Brothers, Bobby Bare, Johnny Lee, and of course, Mickey Gilley and the Urban Cowboy Band.

4

Achy Breaky Heart and Line Dancing

"The dancers hook their thumbs in the front pockets of their jeans and line up shoulder to shoulder. Moving together to the beat . . . a few throw in an extra turn or tip of the hat, but all do their darnedest to exude country cool."
                    —Guy Garcia and Dan Cray, *Time* 1993

Similar to how the memory of the Vietnam War faded by 1980, Americans shied away from the Urban Cowboy fascination by 1990, and movies such as *Urban Cowboy* and the real life Gilley's were just nostalgic memories. The labor required in factories and the oil fields was dwindling as the American workforce shifted its base from a manufacturing to a service economy. By 1992, the U.S. Census reported that over 60 percent of the American workforce worked in service-based jobs. But an unreported amount of hours was the rise in "unpaid" overtime hours and second jobs that most Americans held or were required to perform. In 1987, a Harris Poll reported that the average number of hours worked per week had actually increased from 40.6 in 1973 to 48.4 hours per week (Kraus 1994, 74).

In 1989, a *Time* survey showed that Americans focused more on work than leisure. The magazine claimed, "Americans came to worship career status as a measure of individual worth, and many were willing to sacrifice any amount of leisure time to get ahead." A newly named social class called "Yuppies" generally portrayed the new work ethic.

They were often defined as urban white-collar professionals who were born during the post-World War II Baby Boom generation of 1945 to 1960. In addition, a condition of Yuppies was also attached to working in financial jobs, such as investment banking and the stock market. By conservative numbers, over 20 million were classified as yuppies and being "busy" was advertised as a sign of status. For the most part, the media focused on portraying this group as willing to sacrifice any amount of leisure time in the pursuit of material gain. These classifications grew out of the late 1980s, a period that was sometimes labeled the "Greed Decade," characterized by hostile corporate mergers and acquisitions fostered by the Reagan/Bush presidential years. On the other hand, there were many who held onto a nostalgic memory of dancing and simply relaxing and having fun. Some of that held sway among those that remembered the Country & Western dance craze associated with *Urban Cowboy*.

A New Breed of Urban Cowboy

For many, though, the actual Gilley's did not always hold fond memories. In 1994, for example, Barbara L. Fredricksen, on assignment for the *St. Petersburg Times* in Florida was wary about venturing into a Country & Western dance venue. She noted, "My last foray into the world of country dancing had been more than 15 years ago at Gilley's in Pasadena, Texas, home of the original mechanical bull and inspiration for the 1980 movie *Urban Cowboy*." At the time of her visit she remembered, "In its day, it was a real macho place, full of stoney-eyed couples doing the Texas Two-Step at breakneck speed and beer-gutted men in black hats bellowing the two-word lyrics to Cotton-Eyed Joe." She also remembered lots of smoking, drinking, and "a fair share of fistfights." In short, she said, Gilley's was, "No place for a lady to go alone." In that same manner, she also recalled that not only she, but many others at the time, witnessed the "meanness" of the characters in the movie *Urban Cowboy* and were turned off.

In comparison, author Eve Babitz also did not forget the movie storyline that featured quite a few "mean" male characters who also danced (including "Bud," played by John Travolta). However, in her research for *Two by Two: Tango, Two-Step and the L.A. Night* in contrast to that earlier time, Babitz found a completely different type of person. She wrote with some surprise,

It's hard to imagine a really great two-step dancer who would be mean; the dance is so antithetical to that vibe. The places these people dance are very friendly; it's not cool to be mean, it's not "country." (44)

Nevertheless, those such as Eve Babitz and Barbara L. Fredricksen continued to find a new breed of country dancer.

For her research, Fredrickson put on a "pair of denims" and headed to Pure Country Dance Hall, located at the intersection of State Road 52 and U.S. Highway 19. Unlike her previous experience from 15 years ago, she found "a whole different thing." The difference was the amount of solo line dancing as opposed to the traditional partner dancing of the Urban Cowboy era. Fredricksen went to Pure Country Dance Hall on a Wednesday on a night that advertised as "Ladies Night." At a honky-tonk or regular bar, an advertisement for "Ladies Night" was usually meant to attract men, who in many cases greatly outnumbered the women. In contrast, on the "Ladies Night" at Pure Country Dance Hall, it was completely different. For one, Fredricksen noted, "Out of 200 or so people there, about 80 percent were female, age range 21 to 81, married, single and in-between, and all of them apparently relaxed, happy and having a ball" ("Country Dancing Steps Up Heart, Fun," 1).

Nearby in Tampa Bay, Dan DeWitt, also from the *St. Petersburg Times*, observed similar conditions. He visited Joyland III, which had only recently opened three months earlier. On the outside of the building, DeWitt saw a neon sign with racing lights along the outer edge advertising "Country Music Dancing." The exterior resembled a sleek, stylized barn that looked "like a Las Vegas club set down intact on a gravel lot." Joyland was quite large "about the size of an airplane hangar." On the inside, however, it was a different story. Instead of the glitz often found behind the ostentatious exterior, he found "lines of cooperative patrons" attentively standing behind a line dance instructor. Similar to what Barbara Fredricksen witnessed at Pure Country Dance Hall in St. Petersburg, DeWitt counted, "Perhaps 100 men and women in boots and jeans kicked, shuffled and stomped roughly in sync" (DeWitt, "Boot Scootin' Fun," 1).

All over America similar clubs opened, and literally thousands of instructors taught nightly lessons in bars, community centers, YMCAs, high school gymnasiums, and many others. Kelly Gellette, president of the National Association of Country Western Dance Teachers, who in the previous decade numbered her association membership at 50, counted an "explosion" of new members to almost 2,000 in 1993. Gel-lette reasoned, "It is filling a cultural vacuum left 30 years ago when free-form dancing replaced ballroom dance. Since then, there has been a frustrated need for dance that is not overtly sexual, that has stand-ardized steps and style of dress, that all ages can do together" (DeWitt, "Boot Scootin' Fun," 1).

But fun was the major attraction of both the music and dancing. Maggie Spilner in the health-related magazine *Prevention* proclaimed, "You have to go see country-western dancing in action to know how much fun people are having." Beverly Ott, a line-dance teacher at the Midnight Rose in Quakertown, Pennsylvania, reasoned the appeal might have been towards men in particular. She noted,

> The guys seem to like the ambience of country-western dancing.... There are rules to follow, which makes them feel more secure. They can memorize the steps for whole dances. The dance steps are choreo-graphed, and both the man and the woman know what to do next. That takes a lot of pressure off the guy. (Spilner, "Country-Western 101," 7)

Unlike the 1980s, the new breed of Urban Cowboy approached coun-try dancing on an even larger nationwide scale than ever before in American history. Much of that appeal was attributed to the fact that line dancing was so dominant since it did not require a set partner, but did allow dressing up as a "cowboy" or for the ladies as a "cowgirl" for a night of fun.

The fashion went hand-in-hand with the dancing. Kasper Zeuthen of *The Washington Post* observed the weekly line dance lesson at the Brandywine Volunteer Fire Department in Maryland. The instructor, Bill Cole, was described as "dressed in black boots, blue jeans, a red T-shirt and a black cowboy hat." A necessary tool was a wireless headset microphone so the crowd could not only hear the instructor, but also allow uninterrupted freedom of movement. First time line dancers and the curious usually showed up in casual attire such as khakis and sneakers. However, by the second or third time, they often became "hooked," not only on just the line dancing, but also on wearing "cowboy" gear. Line dancers all over the country started dressing in western wear. Men sported polished belt buckles, denim jeans, and sometimes vests. Women also wore jeans, fringed shirts, and frilly dance dresses. And of course, just about everyone wore cowboy hats

A line dance instructor in full "cowboy gear." Noticeable is a wireless headset microphone. (Photographed by and used by permission of Matthew Giordano.)

and cowboy boots. Some couples took to wearing matching shirts. Some women wore a "boot bracelet" (sort of an exterior ankle bracelet). Many dance halls even provided small shops within the dance hall, and others bought authentic western attire by mail-order catalog from companies such as Shepler's ("Suburban Cowboys," M23).

Garth Brooks and Chris LeDoux

The new breed of Urban Cowboy and country music also coincided with the boom in popular music videos popularized by the likes of Madonna and Michael Jackson on the MTV network. Only a few years before, all genres of music were closely tied in with the video production attached to a newly released single. Country music was no exception. At the time, many credited both the country music and its mainstream crossover to a wider popular listening audience with

Garth Brooks (often simply known as Garth). In 1989, his self-titled first album established him as a new breed of country music superstar.

Born in Tulsa, Oklahoma, on February 7, 1962, Brooks was raised as much on country music as he was on popular American music, including Billy Joel and James Taylor. Unlike many earlier generations of singers, Brooks graduated from Oklahoma State University with a degree in advertising—a factor that was often attributed to his creative marketing techniques throughout his career. Similar to other Country singers (by this time the music was simply known as "Country"), he tirelessly performed in many local bars and honky-tonks. In 1985, he felt confident enough to try his hand in Nashville. It took a few years, and he signed a contract with Capitol Records to release his self-titled debut, *Garth Brooks*, in April 1989 ("Garth and New Country").

The first single released by Garth Brooks was, "Much Too Young (To Feel This Damn Old)" reached the top 10 on the country charts. A memorable line from the song paid tribute to another country singer named Chris LeDoux. The continued success of both Garth Brooks and the song also encouraged country music listeners to "discover" LeDoux. Although he had recorded songs for over a decade, it was not until the 1990s that LeDoux's records received wide airplay. During that time, LeDoux also contributed a fair share of danceable hits, including "Honky Tonk World," "Under This Old Hat," and "Cadillac Ranch," among many others. "Cadillac Ranch" was also remixed as an extended dance version that inspired a popular line dance, appropriately titled the "LeDoux Shuffle."

Garth's most memorable hit, however, was the fourth single released off the album titled "The Dance" and written by Tony Arata. An early performance of the song was in a made-for-television movie, *Nashville Beat* (1989). Both the song and video made #1 on both the country and pop charts. Brooks followed up with his second album *No Fences*, which was one of the top selling country albums of all time, with over 13 million copies sold. He also continued with many more top-of-the-chart singles. The combined success of the first two albums and hit singles was most definitely the spark that brought country music into the national spotlight. In September of 1991, the third album release by Garth Brooks, *Ropin the Wind*, became the first country album in *Billboard* chart history to debut as #1 on the top of the overall pop charts ("Garth and New Country").

As a result of Garth Brooks, many new nontraditional fans were buying, listening, and also dancing to country music. The massive influx of nontraditional new country music converts did not always sit well with old diehards. Ken Peters, manager of Denver's Grizzly Rose, called the new converts to country line dancing "yuppie cowboys." His simple reasoning: "They're the ones who have never been on a horse." Although actually riding a horse certainly did not provide any of the skills for dancing, some old diehards of pure country music were offended by the widespread appeal of nontraditionalists to both country music and dancing (Garcia and Cray, "Scoot Your Booty").

Regardless of the old traditionalists, by the mid-1990s, country music was the most popular radio format in America, with over 40 percent of the American population, estimated at 77 million adults, regularly tuned in. At the time, almost every American household had a radio, with each household averaging almost six radios. By 2000, the total number of commercial radio stations was 10,577 (5,892 FM and 4,685 AM stations); an additional 2,140 were noncommercial FM stations, such as

On August 7, 1997, Garth Brooks created a sensational media blitz by staging a live country music concert in New York City's Central Park. (AFP/Getty Images 52023898.)

college radio stations. By that time, if mainstream Americans had not yet heard of Garth Brooks, they certainly did by 1997. In August of that year, he created a sensational media blitz by staging a live country music concert in New York City's Central Park. On a large outdoor stage he performed in front of an estimated one million fans. The show was simulcast live on HBO to a TV audience of more than 15 million people. By the end of the century, his total CD sales topped 100 million, making him the top-selling individual musical act of the entire 20th century. Propelled by Brooks and other new stars such as Chris LeDoux, George Strait, Alan Jackson, Reba McEntire, and many others, Country music sales outpaced all other genres of music in America ("Garth and New Country"; Giordano 2003, 256).

Country Line Dancing

The sudden surge in appreciation for Country music went hand-in-hand with line dancing. During the 1980s, some line dances were also performed including the Cotton-Eyed Joe (also sometimes by this time Cotton Eye Joe). The most popular line dance of not only the 1990s, but also probably the entire 20th and early 21st century was the Electric Slide. Although not noted specifically as a country dance, nor rooted in country music, the Electric Slide was a popular nationwide line dance that was also accepted in the Country & Western clubs.

The song and the line dance arrived in America almost simultaneously in 1983. At that time Jamaican Reggae artist Marcia Griffiths had released the song "Electric Boogie" and the dance also caused a mild sensation. Griffiths, however, did not take credit for the dance, as she thought that her song only gave a name to a line dance that originated in Washington, D.C., around 1970. It is also quite possible that the name was applied to a variation on a 16-count disco-era line dance named the Hot Chocolate and also the Bus Stop. Regardless, even when the Electric Slide became popular nationwide, it had different regional names. In Memphis, Tennessee, for example, it was the Roller Coaster; in Detroit it was called the Hustle; and in both Dayton, Ohio and New Orleans it was simply called the Bus Stop. In either case, the Electric Slide was a smooth, simple four-wall 18-count line dance that began with a distinctive four-count hop and side shuffle to the right, repeated back to the left, followed by a stylized backward walk with some styled moves and a simple quarter turn. It was fun, simple, easy to learn, easy to follow, and could be danced to many genres of music. It was simple and easily adaptable to many country songs and was often seen performed on television by the entire cast of TNN's *Club Dance.*

For unknown reasons, the Electric Slide did not become a nationwide sensation until 1989, when a remixed dance version of the song and an MTV video was released as *Electric Boogie/Electric Slide.* Even Griffiths was quite surprised and could not fully explain why the almost forgotten song and dance had suddenly become "a cultural phenomenon." By the fall of 1989, it was not unusual for large public gatherings just to do the dance. In October, for example, Washington, D.C., held "Electric Slide Day" with over 3,000 people dancing it continuously for 45 minutes. Griffiths did admit, "It's a simple, happy song with a light reggae feel, not hard-core, just a nice crossover touch. Once you hear it, you gotta move" (Milloy, "The Dance That Would Not Die," B3).

In a short time, the Electric Slide seemed to have replaced the Twist as a crowd favorite at weddings and party celebrations, as well as vacation resorts, cruise ships, senior centers, local schools, and the country music clubs. The country version usually substituted two vine steps at the beginning of the sequence instead of the hop and side shuffle. Although not always called out as the Electric Slide, many Country music dance clubs did a modified line dance called "The Freeze," which was simply the first 16 counts of the Electric slide. The difference in The Freeze is that the quarter turn left was done one count earlier and a country-style heel scuff completed the turn. In the Electric Slide that same quarter turn was done on the last two counts, ending with a simultaneous toe touch and hand clap.

The Electric Slide was also a popular Country standard at the Denim & Diamonds country dance franchise. In March 1993, journalists Guy Garcia and Dan Cray from *Time* visited the Denim & Diamonds in Santa Monica, California, on a Saturday night. Unlike what they expected from a Country music dance hall they said, "the joint is jumping." In the past, that phrase was often associated with the likes of swing music, jitterbug, and Rock 'n' Roll, certainly not with dancing to Country & Western music. At one point the dancers performed the Electric Slide. Garcia and Cray described it as follows,

As a band pumps out a country hit, the dancers hook their thumbs in the front pockets of their jeans and line up shoulder to shoulder. Moving together to the beat, they cross one foot over the other and take three steps to the left, three steps to the right, rock back and forth on their heels and kick high. Egged on by hoots and hollers, a few throw in an extra turn or tip of the hat, but all do their darnedest to exude country cool.

During the course of the evening, Garcia and Cray also watched other country line dances including the Walkin' Wazi, Boot Scootin' Boogie, Honky-Tonk Stomp, and the Tush Push, among many others. By the early 1990s, there were many variations of all sorts of line dances, as well as variations on the basic Electric Slide ("Scoot Your Booty").

A similar country line dance with a slight variation from the Electric Slide was the "Electric Horseman," which was often danced to the Garth Brooks song "We Shall Be Free." The Electric Horseman brought the dance to 24 counts and added some delayed foot stomps prior to the quarter-turn. In essence, many of the line dances built on others combining similar steps or adding new ones to familiar patterns. Another example, with a slight variation on the Electric Slide, was the Cowboy Boogie. It had similar movements that replaced the hop and a skip from the Electric Slide with a very country modified vine step and heel scuffs. All in all, the Electric Slide was extremely popular across the nation, as was the Macarena.

In 1993, the song and the 16-count hand-dance Macarena was also a nationwide sensation that was often welcomed at parties in conjunction with the Electric Slide. In fact, in the mid-1990s, both were almost inseparable during any party or catered event. It was a simple dance that was almost all hand and arm movements. Many clubs, parties, and organizations held Macarena nights, even in major league baseball stadiums. It was also popular with the country line dancers, but as just one among many favorites. During the country line dance craze of the 1990s, the Tush Push was probably the most well-known and most favored of all the country line dances. The country line dance craze of the 1990s, however, was not the result of any previous dance, nor for that matter influenced by a Hollywood movie, but rather it was launched by one song in particular.

Achy Breaky Heart

In 1992, the song "Achy Breaky Heart" (written by Don Von Tress) on the debut album by Billy Ray Cyrus kicked off a nationwide country line dance craze. The album, *Some Gave All* on the Nashville Mercury label, was boosted by the popularity of the song, and in a short time sold over 11 million copies. Actually, the song "Achy Breaky Heart" was released as a single about five weeks in advance of the album release and was an immediate hit selling 500,000 copies. The mega-success also crossed over to popular music as *Some Gave All* was not only at the top of the country charts, but also #1 on the *Billboard* pop album chart for four consecutive weeks. In July 1992, *The New York Times* described Cyrus as, "He has come out of nowhere to become the biggest pop-music phenomenon of the moment." For some, both Cyrus and country dancing might have appeared to come "out of nowhere," but "Achy Breaky Heart" was the catalyst that opened up the Country music radio airwaves to mainstream audiences and also introduced many to country line dancing. Unbeknownst to many, however, was that Cyrus, 30 years old at the time of *Some Gave All*, had toiled for almost 12 years "playing virtually every night" in all sorts honky-tonks and bars (Watrous, "He's Hot and Not Just to Fans of Country," C15; Schoemer, "A Pop Star Shining in the Glow of Success," C13).

Ironically for the person that launched a new dance craze, Cyrus was definitely not a dancer, but on-stage he did have a distinctive hip-swinging move. For the dance, choreographer Melanie Greenwood built off of that move, and of course the song, to create a line dance called the Achy Breaky. The dance was first performed for the promotional music video released on March 6, 1992, coinciding with the release of the song. In connection with the music video, an instructional video for the Achy Breaky was sent to Country & Western dance clubs all across the nation. As Greenwood described in the video, "It's three hips left, right, left, sort of an Elvis thing." The videotaped instruction was also part of a national promotional Achy Breaky dance contest. In a few months the song and the dance were just about everywhere. In August 1992, for example, *The New York Times* offered the dance instruction in a Sunday feature titled, "Achy Breaky: A 22-step line-dance sensation with Billy Ray Cyrus's cheatin'-heart No. 1 single" (Patton, V8).

Both the song and Cyrus had an indescribable appeal that was catchy, fun, and certainly likeable. In turn, the request for the song in the Country & Western dance clubs prompted dancers to replicate the same Greenwood dance from the video. Prompted by the Achy Breaky, she choreographed three other exclusive dances for other artists. They included the country Lambada for Lorrie Morgan's song "Watch Me," the Four Star Boogie for the song "Now That's Country," a hit for Marty Stuart, and a humorously titled Stretchin' Denim for "Jealous Bone," by Patty Loveless. During that same year, Greenwood also released two instructional videos. The first, *Hot Country Dancin'*, was a re-release of a video from 1981 and the second *Hot Country Dancin' Vol. 2* followed on the success of the Achy Breaky. Both were published by Reel Productions in Nashville ("Music swings toward Foot-Stomping Beats," 5D).

With the success of "Achy Breaky Heart," all sorts of new line dances were choreographed in the hopes of promoting a particular song with the same success. In an attempt to capitalize on the fad, many record companies and radio stations staged promotional events. In March 1993, *Billboard* offered a page one headline,

> Country stations looking for ways to connect with their fans as well as win over new ones are heading to local clubs with growing regularity in search of line-dancing enthusiasts.

At station WNOE-FM New Orleans, programming director Dave Nicholson suggested a Saturday night three-hour live broadcast from a local club. Nicholson was inspired by the effect of "Achy Breaky Heart," and his idea was to capitalize on the line dance craze and promote a "commercial-free dance party." From week to week, a different WNOE on-air personality passed out promotional material in conjunction with a dance contest in various clubs in the New Orleans vicinity. Often the dance contest was tied to the promotion of a new song release by a specific country artist. Sometimes the promotion was to develop a new line dance for a new song. Many other radio stations did the same.

In March 1993, WOW-FM in Omaha, Nebraska and WKKX in St. Louis, Missouri, each took part in a "simultaneous, multi market record-release party." The occasion was a new single "Honky Tonk Walkin' " by the Kentucky Headhunters. The idea was for listeners to come up with a new dance to match the song. In turn, the radio station provided prizes for the participants. According to Gary Dick, president of an entertainment marketing firm, it was a simple opportunity for the radio station "to pick up more listeners." At the same time, the record label was able to "spotlight" a particular artist, which resulted in a boost in record sales (Boehlert, "Country Stations Step to the Line to Woo New Listeners," 80).

Although line dancing, beginning around 1990, was gaining in popularity, it was mainly due to the phenomenal success of "Achy Breaky Heart" that country line dancing caught on all across America— especially in the big cities where country music and dancing was not considered traditional. At about the same time, the music and dancing was no longer called Country & Western: it was simply called "Country." Also, Country music was gaining in national popularity as was Country & Western dancing featured on television shows reminiscent of *American Bandstand*.

Club Dance and the White Horse Cafe

In 1989, *American Bandstand* ended a remarkable string of 37 years on local, network, and cable television. For 32 of those years, Dick Clark was the host, and both he and the show became an indelible part of American culture. The show did not require any deep analysis. Simply put, *American Bandstand* spotlighted teenagers dancing to the latest trend in music. Although it was immensely popular and influential by introducing mainstream America to such dance styles as Rock 'n' Roll, the Twist, freestyle, and disco, it never did promote Country & Western dancing. A few years after the end of *American Bandstand*, another television dance show did introduce Country & Western dancing to a wide audience.

On April 1, 1991, *Club Dance* first aired on The Nashville Network (TNN). David Zimmerman, in an article for *USA Today*, called the show "Country music's version of Rock 'n' Roll's old American Bandstand." For the most part, the one-hour long show was quite similar to *American Bandstand*, featuring nonstop dancing to the prerecorded music of contemporary country artists. Occasionally an older "classic" might be played. And from time to time a Country music artist stopped by for a short interview, promoting a new song. Often a music video would be played, but usually it was relegated to one of the many TV screens located along the back walls as the TV cameras concentrated on those who were dancing.

But the show had a slow start. TNN contracted for at least 65 shows scheduled to be shown over 13 consecutive weeks, but during the first few tapings attendance was sporadic. In fact, the first rehearsals had only five couples, and by the first show a total of only 27 people. At one taping only 17 dancers were in the studio and during the first few weeks the show only averaged about 20 dancers. An anxious senior producer, Cynthia Scott, seeking to fill the studio, quickly borrowed a blank cue card, wrote in big letters, "Dancers Wanted! Follow Me To Studio!" and stood alongside a busy highway. She also scoured some local clubs looking for anyone interested in dancing on the show. It took a few months, but word spread and eventually a mix of about 50 or 60 regulars continually showed up, and each show let in about another 200 to 300 visitors who also danced. They all ranged in age from teenagers to seniors. None of the dancers received any pay for their appearances on the show. One regular said they were all there for "the love of country dance." A review of the show in *TV Guide* reported, "Those are real people. They're not here for publicity. They're here for the fun." *Club Dance* caught on and shortly thereafter, the show's producers had to turn down hundreds of request. At one point there was a waiting list for guests of over six months. Remembering those early days, host Shelley Mangrum said, "we were just glad to get people in the studio" (Stuart, 14–16).

The early shows featured Shelley Mangrum as host within the studio-designed setting of a fictitious bar named the "White Horse Cafe." It was that association that had at first named the show *Club Dance at the Whitehorse Cafe*. A short time later, after a mild dispute with a local venue of a similar name, the name was changed to just *Club Dance*. The set itself was designed by Cinetel's art director Randy Armstrong to incorporate elements as if it were a converted barn reminiscent of an old-fashioned barn dance. Duncan Mansfield of the *Associated Press* described the simple set as "basically a large sunken dance floor surrounded by a brass railing with tables and chairs for the sitters and watchers." The studio set was complete with a dance floor, various levels of seating, and a bar with a friendly bartender. From April 1991 through 1993, Cotton Perrin was the "bartender" set on an upper level. Due to his untimely death in 1993, Phil Campbell replaced him. A separate raised area was usually reserved for line dancers or swing dancers. The main lower level was usually packed with Two-stepping couples as Shelley roamed about talking to the "customers." The idea lessened the approach of interviewing any Country music stars and focused attention on the "lives and events of everyday people" (Stuart, 16–26).

Similar to *American Bandstand*, the real stars of the show were the everyday non-professional dancers. Unlike the teenage dance party of *American Bandstand*, the regulars on *Club Dance* appealed to all age groups, mainly because those on the show were also of varying ages. And it was that appeal that had viewers tuning in just to follow the regulars and their daily lives. In response, co-hosts Shelley Mangrum and Phil Campbell played up the personal relationships. Mangrum was familiar to TNN viewers as she had previously hosted the TNN music video show, *Video Country* in 1983, and later *Video Gold*. Phil Campbell was also known among Country & Western music fans as a former cast member of *Hee-Haw*. He first joined the show in 1993, during a Christmas week break for Shelley, and later after the death of Perrin, Campbell was soon asked to co-host with Mangrum. But it did not take long for Campbell to understand, "The real stars are the dancers." (Stuart, 31).

In response to the interest in *Club Dance*, Mangrum proclaimed, "I had no idea there were so many people out there who enjoyed country dancing and enjoyed watching country dancing." Apparently, network executives sensed the correct timing of the nationwide rise in country music. In September of 1991, as *Ropin the Wind* the third album by Garth Brooks was released, *Club Dance* had been on-air for six months. The following year Billy Ray Cyrus released his debut album *Some Gave All* and also appeared on *Club Dance* on September 2, 1992. At the time he was basically an "unknown" billed as an up-and-coming artist. A few months later, his single "Achy Breaky Heart" was released and by the time Cyrus returned to *Club Dance* on April 14, 1993, he was well-known not only in the country music world, but also among country dancers. On that show he performed "Achy Breaky Heart," and the crowd danced along (Stuart, 94; Zimmerman, "Country Dancing Keeps in Step with Modern Times,"5D).

Within this environment, *Club Dance* was averaging as many as one million viewers. In 1994, the contract extended for 265 shows and soon thereafter continued each year through the 1990s. It was during those first few years that two shows were taped on Thursday, three on Friday, and four shows on Saturday. Later, two to three episodes were taped each day on both Friday and Saturday. The shooting schedule usually ran from April through August, filming as many episodes as necessary to fill up the year. The episodes aired each weekday, Monday through Friday at 6:30 p.m., and repeated at 10:30 p.m. (EST). As the show's popularity grew, TNN added an additional weekday telecast at 2:00 p.m. of a show from the previous year. After the filming, the regulars usually went out dancing.

And it was the featured group of about 60 regular dancers that the viewers wanted to know about. The idea was to keep the music playing and dancers on the floor. As it was all going on, both Mangrum and Campbell would do a few quick interviews with both the regulars and even those who drove sometimes hundreds of miles to appear on the show. Oftentimes, the guests celebrated special events such as birthdays, anniversaries, and even honeymoons. Viewers soon found out that quite a few regulars such as Cindy V., Ray A., and Geneva A. were single; and others such as Johnny and Janie A. and Sam and Linda H. were married. Some, such as Bob and Paula, who were single, first met on the show in 1992 and later married during a taping of the show on April 20, 1996. The "Wedding Show," was aired on May 23, 1996, and the at-home viewers loved the real-life drama. The drama played out with others who were dating, having an argument, looking for an apartment, taking time off for a baby, announcing an engagement, a break-up, divorce, unemployment, layoffs, as well as getting a new job, among many other types of real-life issues. In response, the regulars also received over 750 fan letters each month. Shelley recalled, "Around the time we began playing up the soap opera, the viewers started picking up. . . . It all kind of clicked at the same time" (Stuart, 26, 38–39).

If viewers could not get enough from the TV show, they could get even more information by subscribing to a monthly newsletter. The first *Club Dance Newsletter* of February 1994 promised, "The inside story on Cable Television's Most Famous Country & Western Dance Club." The seventh anniversary 12-page newsletter featured a cast photo of almost 60 regulars and proclaimed that *Club Dance* "is a celebration of life for all those who enjoy dancing to the throbbing beat of country music." Within that newsletter was also a merchandise catalog for T-shirts, denim jackets, glasses, key chains, buttons, hats, watches, duffle bags, a coffee mug, bean bag bear, and instructional dance videos—all with the official *Club Dance* logo. The show also launched all sorts of other promotions. In May 1996, for example, a launch of the NASA space shuttle *Endeavour* carried along a *Club Dance* hat worn by astronaut Col. John Casper. In 1998, Cinetel Productions and TNN also commissioned Nancy Rubin Stuart to author a commemorative seventh anniversary book titled *Club Dance Scrapbook: The Show, The Steps, The Spirit of Country* (Stuart, 4, 7, 77).

The "White Horse Cafe" might have been a fictional place created for television, but many viewers thought it was a real Country &

John and Toby Johnson, center, of Decatur, Michigan, during taping of the last "Club Dance" show January 23, 1999 in Knoxville, Tennessee. The Johnsons made the 550-mile drive to "Club Dance" about twice a month since 1992. The final taping was the 1,849th installment of the show and aired February 5, 1999. (Courtesy Paul Efird, Knoxville News Sentinel.)

Western dance venue. Although *Club Dance* was filmed on a set in a television studio in Knoxville, Tennessee, director Ross Bagwell, Jr. said, "People believe it's a real place, and it is a real place to the people who come here. They don't think of it as a television studio." The fact that the White Horse was fictional was even announced during one of the shows. Host Shelley Mangrum interviewed three women who had driven up from Jacksonville, Florida in search of the dance hall. After an exhaustive search that included looking through the telephone directory and questioning local individuals, one motel clerk told them that it was a TV show filmed nearby at the Cinetel Productions studios. During the interview, producer Cindy White leaned to a reporter from the *Associated Press* and said, "It's unbelievable the lengths that some people will go to find out where the White Horse is." Therefore, the misconception of reality necessitated a press release from TNN to say that the "honky-tonk doesn't exist." The network further explained, "It's only a soundstage in a gleaming white mirrored building on the Nashville side of Knoxville" (Mansfield, "Nashville Sound: Cable Show Has 'em Two-Steppin' ").

However, as with all good things—or more appropriately, sometimes nationwide sensations—*Club Dance* ended its seven-year run in February 1999. At the time the network, owned by CBS, changed its program format as well as its name to The National Network, and later to SpikeTV. It was somewhat bittersweet that Duncan Mansfield of the *Associated Press*, who had covered the first show in April 1991 and wrote the article "Nashville Sound: Cable Show Has 'em Two-Steppin'," also had the unfortunate distinction of writing a final article on *Club Dance*, sadly titled, "Last dance at popular Nashville TV club."

The Wildhorse Saloon

During its heyday, the success of *Club Dance* was enough for Cinetel Productions to spin-off a similar show named *Dance Line*. It was also aired on TNN, featuring dance instructor Jo Thompson as the host and some *Club Dance* regulars. However, it did not last long. On the other hand, unlike *Club Dance* which was filmed in a studio, another TNN dance show was filmed in an actual country music dance hall named the Wildhorse Saloon. In 1994, TNN programmed the country dance show named *The Wildhorse Saloon* hosted by Katie Haas and later Bobby Randall. (The original title was *"Live at the Wildhorse Saloon,"* but, later the shows were taped in a similar fashion to *Club Dance*.) The dance show was filmed in the actual Wildhorse Saloon that had opened that same year in Nashville, Tennessee. The three-story red brick building was centered on a 3,300 square foot dance floor that could hold over 1,000 dancers and boasted over one million visitors each year. It offered a combination of live stage shows and DJ country music. The Wildhorse was open seven days a week, with free dance lessons from 7:00 p.m. to 9:00 p.m. during the week and also offered an hourly dance lesson from 2:00 p.m. to 9:00 p.m. on Saturdays and Sundays (http://www.Wildhorsesaloon.com).

The TV show was filmed during the late afternoon and into early evening hours. At first a television film crew set up in the actual Wildhorse to film five shows between the hours of 7:00 p.m. and 10:00 p.m. twice each week. Unlike *Club Dance*, any individual could show up to be in the audience and also simply take part in the filming by just going onto the floor to dance. The 60-minute show interspersed interviews with Country music artists as well as dance instruction

The Wildhorse Saloon in Nashville, Tennessee, opened in 1994 in a three-story red brick building with a 3,300 square foot dance floor and attracted over one million customers each year. The TNN country-dance show *The Wildhorse Saloon* hosted by Katie Haas was also filmed there. (Associated Press photograph by Christopher Berkey 1371552.)

segments, and of course time out for commercials. From time to time, guest instructors such as Barry Durand and Jo Thompson appeared for quick dance segments. Similar to *Club Dance*, it also aired each weekday, but at 5:00 p.m. (EST). In 1997, Maureen Needham attended the Wildhorse in preparation for an article in *The Nashville Scene*. In regards to those that appeared on the TV show, she noted,

> The experience offers a brief glimpse of fame and glory to anyone who takes the trouble to show up on a weekday night and learn a few steps in tandem before stepping out in front of the cameras. (84)

Dancing "in tandem" was certainly a big part of the country dancing element, but the major appeal nationwide was still country line dancing.

Country Line Dancing

Some early converts, such as Judy Dygdon and Tony Conger, first discovered line dancing early in 1990 at a country dance in Houma, Louisiana, located southeast of New Orleans in Bayou country. As with many others, they misunderstood that they were going to a "country club," assuming it was the kind associated with a private golf course. Coincidentally the name of the music club was also "The Country Club." Much to their surprise, and eventual enjoyment, it was a "Country music club" replete with partner, round, and line dancing. They described their first time ever seeing country line dancing as follows,

> A Country and Western song began and, as we watched in amazement, the dance floor filled with people in regimented lines, and they were all doing exactly the same thing! We looked at each other and instantly knew that we had to learn more about this. . . . we wanted to line dance." (1)

One of the main appeals of country line dancing, not only to Dygdon and Conger, but also to thousands of others just like them, was that a person did not need a partner to dance. It was similar to freestyle dancing in the sense that an individual did not need a dedicated partner holding hands, but could just go out on the dance floor and join in a group. Similar to freestyle dancing, anyone of any age could mix on the dance floor, both young and old, and it was especially conducive to single and widowed people.

A distinguishing style that set country line dancing, and for that matter, also partner dancing, apart from other dance styles, such as freestyle, was the arms, or more appropriately, the lack of the use of the arms. As Dygdon and Conger pointed out in *Country & Western Line Dancing*, "Cowboys [and cowgirls] do not flail or dangle their arms—even when doing spins or turns" (6). During a line dance, for example, women were instructed to place both of their hands behind their backs. Also discouraged was placing hands on the hips such as in folk, the Irish jig, or step dance fashion. In similar fashion, men either were told that they could place their thumbs inside the top of their jeans while holding the outside of their belt buckle. For many, the fashionable style was a large decorative belt buckle, therefore, there was certainly enough to hold onto. An alternative was to place their thumbs in their front hip pockets.

Unlike freestyle dancing, line dancing was regimented, structured, and organized, with all the participants attempting to perform the same steps in unison and move in the same coordinated direction. Dygdon and Conger provided a simple concise description as, "Country and Western line dances are sequences of steps that form a pattern. Line dancing is done by repeating the pattern for a duration of a piece of music" (8). Prior to starting any particular dance pattern, the DJ (or sometimes a band member) called out the name of an upcoming dance. If the dancers knew it, they headed onto the dance floor, or in many cases stayed after completing the previous dance. During the musical prelude, as the dancers were queued up, they waited for a DJ prompt counting out "5, 6, 7, 8." In doing so, the group was able to start in unison.

Most of the line dances were matched to the song phrasing in set patterns of 16-, 24-, 32-, or 48-count patterns. The prompt of 5, 6, 7, 8, was important to both begin the line dancers in unison and within the proper rhythm of a particular song. The count matched the solid 4/4 beat of most country songs such as the Two Step, Swing, or Cha Cha. In a country Waltz rhythm, the start count was changed to 4, 5, 6. Each of the line dances were also defined as either a one-wall, two-wall, or four-wall dance. The "wall" designation meant that at the predetermined 16-, 24-, 32, or 48-count pattern the line dancer starting the new sequence might be facing a different wall. The line dance queue was suggested to begin facing "the front," which could be, depending on club policy, the bandstand, the bar, or even the DJ booth. In the absence of a bandstand, or for that matter an actual band, a DJ orientated the crowd, and in most cases cued the crowd to start on the familiar phrase of "5, 6, 7, 8." Most of the cueing was based on beginning the song with the lyrics as the line dances were choreographed to match the rhythm and phrasing of the particular song or rhythm.

A one-wall dance might have involved a turn or two, but the begin and end sequence always remained forward, or to "the front." The wall in a complete 180-degree direction from the predetermined "front" was described as "the back." On the other hand, for a two-wall dance, the new sequence would begin in a complete 180-degree direction of the dance floor, or facing "the back." A four-wall dance typically started each sequence facing a new wall at a 90-degree turn each time. Therefore, a four-wall dance meant that each sequence began facing each of the four walls of the dance club. At the beginning of the line dance craze, most were one and two wall dances and the patterns were arranged from very simple to basic.

Most of the basic or "beginner level" line dances matched one step with one beat of music in 24-count and 32-count sequences, devoid of any syncopations or complicated turns. The turns were usually an introduction to a basic quarter-turn, so as not to totally disorientate the dancer. As the fad exploded, the number of dances increased by the thousands, as did the varying degrees from simple one-wall dances with no turns and a few steps to very complex four-wall dances with many turns and syncopations within the set dance sequence. Sometimes the complex dance steps would increase the pattern sequence to 64 counts, or in some cases 96 counts, and more and even more difficult skill levels. In all cases, they set up in line formation, which was sometimes called "military drill formation." In order to keep the uniformity and proper spacing between the other line dancers Dygdon and Conger suggested,

> When you do line dancing, it is important to remember that part of the beauty of these dances is the regularity of lines. When you join a dance on the floor, make sure you are: facing the same direction as the other dancers, positioned squarely behind the person in front of you, and in a straight line with the people next to you. (5)

Regardless of the reminder, everyone who attended a Country music club or who took any instruction at all quickly learned the rules.

Learning the Line Dances

Many learned the line dances by arriving at the dance club early in the evening. Usually an instructor was hired by the venue offering two dance lessons free with the cover charge. The dances were practiced to two or three songs of varying speeds and were repeated once or twice during the evening. The steps were usually provided on pre-printed sheets and handed out at the end of the lessons. Others learned the line dances in private studios, community centers, local schools, senior centers, YMCAs, and other venues. Country line dancing became so popular and was available at so many other places that many never even had to go to a honky-tonk or music club to dance.

The written step descriptions accompanied by verbal instruction also introduced the participants to a new language of dance. Some of the terms included a hitch, pivot, vine step, heel-toe, heel-hook, triple-step, coaster step, and kick-ball-change, among many others. For example, instructors often described using the "ball" of the foot in a "kick-ball-change." The "triple-step" was the term often applied as a non-technical application of the chassé step. Country dance instructors also often called it a syncopated "one and two" when a cha cha step was desired.

Some of the more common line dances included the Ski Bumpus, the Cowboy Boogie, Waltz Across Texas, Electric Cowboy, Foot Boogie, and Cowboy Rhythm. They were fairly standard and often danced the same way across the country. On the other hand, many line dances either became wedded to, or were written for only one specific song. Two of the most common were "Trashy Women" by Confederate Railroad, and "Watermelon Crawl" by Tracy Byrd. In the case of "Trashy

In this 1995 photo, an instructor and his partner teach the El Paso partner dance at the Pony Express in Staten Island, New York. The couples are side-to-side in a "cape position." (Author's Archives.)

Women," when the song first came out, dancers performed an appropriately matched line dance known as Horsin' Around. The dance fit the song so well, however, that the name of the dance soon became universally known as Trashy Women. On the other hand, some popular dances such as Fallsview Rock were consistent nationwide, but often danced to a variety of different songs. This dance was named after the Fallsview Hotel in Ellenville, New York, where the dance was premiered during a country dance weekend.

The more popular partner dances included the El Paso, Wooden Nickel, Kansas City Four Corners, Blue Rose, Sweetheart Schottische, and the Cowboy Cha Cha (also known as the Traveling Cha Cha). Most of the partner dances began with a couple in a side by side "cape position." It was named that because the man's hands were placed above and behind the woman's shoulders, as if was putting a cape on her. The woman held both arms up, palms outward and held hands with the man right hand to right hand and left hand to left hand. Other fixed pattern partner dances with various handholds included the Charleston Bump, Shadow, and the Sidekick. People of the same gender could do some of the fixed pattern partner dances side-by-side or without a partner that included the Ten-step and the 16-Step. Partner dances that traveled along the perimeter included the Two Step, Waltz, and Triple-step. The traditional slow dance among couples was known as a "Buckle Polisher." Many of the dances could be seen on televised dance shows, or learned from VHS tapes or instruction books.

The ability to learn country line dancing was not limited to any of the dance halls or community centers. Anyone wishing to learn country dancing could do so within the comfort of their own home with the purchase of an instructional video playable on a Video Cassette Recorder (VCR) and television. They could choose from many of hundreds of mail-order instructional dance videos. One distribution group in particular, Quality Video, based in Minneapolis, Minnesota, shipped 650,000 copies between September 1992 and February 1993. By March 1993, they were mailing out instructional videos at a rate of about 100,000 a month. Other examples included the official *Club Dance Instructional Dance Video* produced by Cinetel. Series 1 included instruction for the Two Step and Waltz filmed in the actual *Club Dance* studio. *Country Dancing Made Easy* with Jerry Staeheli featured the Two Step. He also had other videos for the West Coast Swing,

Anyone wishing to learn country dancing could do so within the comfort of their own home with the purchase of an instructional video. Two shown here are *Denim & Diamonds Favorite Line Dances* (left) and *Country Dancing Made Easy* with Jerry Staeheli featuring the Two Step (right). (Author's Archives.)

Ten-Step, Waltz and four volumes to learn country line dancing. Denim & Diamonds also released *Favorite Line Dances*, featuring instructions for Boot Scootin' Boogie, Cowboy Cha Cha, Electric Slide, and the Tush Push (Garcia and Cray, "Scoot Your Booty").

One instructional book was *The Big Book of Country Western Dancing*, by Nancy and Aubrey Woodroof. It was a compendium of over 500 Country Line dances arranged in alphabetical order and grouped in different levels of difficulty. Classifications were ranked for beginners, intermediate, advanced, and a few as challenging. About 100 of the list were easy to learn and for beginners. Within the basic ratings was also a graded system of one to five stars. A one-star rating was for a Beginner. A two-star dance was a Beginner/Intermediate, and four-stars was Intermediate/Advanced. Five-stars was the most challenging. One example of a "Beginner Line Dance" was the Cowboy Boogie. A typical instruction step sheet for the Cowboy Boogie was as follows,

Cowboy Boogie

DESCRIPTION: 24-count, 4-WALL BEGINNER LINE DANCE

SUGGESTED MUSIC: *The Big One* by George Strait (slow); *Dancing in a Sea of Cowboy Hats* by Chely Wright (medium); *All You Ever Do is Bring Me Down* by The Mavericks (fast); *Cowboy Boogie* by Randy Travis (fast).

BEAT/STEP DESCRIPTION:

VINE RIGHT, VINE LEFT, FORWARD SCUFF, BACKWARD WALK

1 – 4   Vine Step Right, Cross and Step Left Over Right, Step Side Right, Scuff Left Heel Forward.

5 – 8   Vine Step Left, Cross and Step Right Over Left, Step Side Left, Scuff Right Heel Forward.

9 – 12   Step Forward Right, Scuff Left Heel Forward, Step Forward Left, Scuff Right Heel Forward.

14 – 16   Step Back Right, Left, Right, Left.

HIP BUMPS, QUARTER TURN

17 – 18   With Weight on Left Foot and Bump Left Hip Twice.

19 – 20   Shift Weight to Right and Bump Right Hip Twice.

21 – 22   Shift Weight to Left and Bump Left Hip Once, Shift Weight to Right and Bump Right Hip Once.

23 – 24   Step Left beginning Quarter-turn to Left, Complete Quarter-turn with Right Heel Scuff.

(Note: Right Heel is up Ready to Begin Again with a Vine Step Right).

These sheets are as they existed and were not always grammatically correct.

The hundreds of line dances, however, were both a blessing and a curse for those who simply loved the country dancing. The initial appeal of both country line dancing and partner was the simplicity. However, with the continued attachment of line dancing to Country music songs, the amount of different line and choreographed couple dances multiplied dramatically. In a short time, just about every new country song also had its own specific choreographed line dance, couple dance, or in quite a few cases, one each for the same song. The task of trying to memorize the steps to the 500 or so dances as listed in publications such as *The Big Book of Country Western Dancing* was daunting enough. But the onslaught created by literally thousands of choreographed dances was out of control. Added to the mix was that many dance clubs nationwide choreographed their own line dances specific only to their venue. One example was the Denim & Diamonds chain, which had its own version of Boot Scootin Boogie, Tumbleweed, and Cheatin' Heart, among others.

Some of the country dances suggested a variety of appropriate songs for a particular dance. However, many others suggested only one song for a particular dance, usually of the same name such as "Baby Likes to Rock-It," "Watermelon Crawl," "Trashy Women," "All My Ex's Live In Texas," "Bubba Hyde," "Copperhead Road," "Funky Cowboy," "Boot Scootin' Boogie," "Achy Breaky Heart," "God Blessed Texas," "Honky Tonk Twist," "Long Legged Hannah," "Jose Cuervo," and "Reggae Cowboy," just to name a very few. But some, such as "All Shook Up," only suggested a song that was a specific cover version, in this case by Billy Joel from the *Honeymoon in Vegas* soundtrack and not the original by Elvis Presley. However, the line dance, which was greeted with joy by swing dancers, was complicated. It consisted of three different sequences arranged as A B, A B C, A B C, A B A—with A at 32 counts, B at 28 counts, and C with 16 counts of music.

In other instances, Kaw-Liga was a dance that was most often done to the song of the same name recorded by both Hank Williams, Sr. and Jr. In the early 1950s, Hank Sr. had recorded his original version and during the 1990s, Hank Jr. recorded it also with an attachment to a country line dance. However, it stirred some controversy among some Native American groups. The song told of Kaw-Liga, a wooden Indian that stood outside a tobacco store, and that riled those opposed to the stereotyping of Native Americans. Shortly thereafter, Tim McGraw released "Indian Outlaw," loosely borrowing from the 1960s Paul Revere hit "Cherokee Nation." Both McGraw's song and the Williams song were choreographed to a dance of the same name, "Indian Outlaw," and in some regions, "Indian Runner." Some mild opposition to the dance arose; however, as the songs faded from the music charts, so did the dance and also the opposition.

In *The Big Book of Country Western Dancing*, Nancy and Aubrey Woodroof advertised "at least 504" known dances and, "The most complete collection of country western line dances available in a single book" (back cover). However, by the time of publication in 1996, there were thousands of variations already available. One constant, however, was the listing of "Dance Floor Courtesy and Etiquette." The basic rules as outlined by the Woodroofs were almost the same in every venue that offered Country & Western dancing. They wrote,

For the comfort of others on the dance floor:

- Do not stand on the dance floor to socialize. If you are not dancing, move off the dance floor.
- Do not take food or drinks onto the dance floor.
- If you bring small children, encourage them to dance with the group, but be sure to teach them dance floor etiquette. Running and sliding on the dance floor is dangerous.

For everyone's comfort on the dance floor:

- If you collide on the dance floor, it doesn't matter who is at fault. A smile and sincere apology is in order.
- If you see newcomers on the dance floor, offer to help them. Let them know where and when lessons are given in your area (Woodroof, xvii).

Just about everywhere, the "Line of Dance" was continually stressed as the couple and partner dances progressed counterclockwise along the perimeter. The line dancers were in the center of the floor and the swing dancers on the corners, or sometimes at the rear of the line dancers, but inside the progressive couple dancers. In many cases the DJ would make periodic announcements as to the dance floor rules. Oftentimes it was witnessed that a DJ would step down on the dance floor and politely remind an interloper of the courtesy. In some errant cases it was inevitable that one, or even a few individuals (often with a drink or bottle of beer in hand) would interfere, and a bouncer would move them off the floor. Regardless of the venue, rural or urban, dance floor etiquette and proper decorum was strongly encouraged. Many establishments and instructors handed out lists of the "rules" of the dance floor at the door.

Judy Dygdon and Tony Conger, in *Country & Western Line Dancing: Step-by-Step Instructions for Cowgirls & Cowboys*, presented a thorough explanation providing many dances in a variety of descriptions such as queuing tools, rhythm line, description of the steps, combinations, and individual steps in sequential numbering. Although initially written to introduce England to American Country & Western line dancing, it was quite helpful at home. They also arranged the book in ascending level of difficulty, adding a new step or combination gradually throughout the 50-plus dances. Dygdon and Conger also documented and encouraged "variations" within the set step patterns. They wrote,

> Part of the fun of line dancing for many people is the challenge of mastering specific steps and combinations. If you are one of those people, we attempt to add to your challenge and to your fun. . . . A variation might be a new way to do a combination, perhaps adding a turn, or a replacement set of more difficult steps. It isn't necessary for you to try the variations, but they are there for you to explore. (9)

Variations were usually employed in those specific dances that were most popular and also danced once or twice every night. The best example was the "Tush Push" a dance that remained a favorite from 1980 through the 1990s and into the 21st century.

The Tush Push was probably the most well-known of all the country line dances. It was danced in 4/4 time to mostly country songs that had a swing or Rock 'n' Roll type beat. Jim Ferrazanno wrote the Tush Push combining single step patterns and syncopated cha cha steps as a 40-count, 4-wall intermediate line dance. In fact, Ferrazanno originally wrote the Tush Push for non-country music. Throughout America, in both rural honky-tonks and big city country dance clubs, just about every country dancer knew the Tush Push, or at the very least knew of it. And almost everywhere it was done exactly the same. The reason could be attributed to the fact that the dance was written in 1980 and the steps were published and distributed in clubs and instruction studios well before the line dance craze began. Another reason could be that it was seen almost daily on television country dance shows such as *Club Dance* and *The Wildhorse Saloon*, which featured the Tush Push almost every day of the week. One exception was in Charleston, South Carolina, with a variation of the Tush Push at 39 counts combining the stomp and clap of two beats at the end of the sequence into one. The South Carolina version was "off-sequence" to the music and therefore not easily conducive to variations.

More than any other country line dance, the Tush Push was often individualized with variations. In all likelihood, since it was danced so much and therefore, the dancers were comfortable with it, they could then include variation without losing the rhythm. Most of the Tush Push variations were observed during the first eight-count, as the heel-together-heel-switch was replaced with variations such as heel twists or swivels, or jumping feet apart, crossing the legs and turning around for the first four counts and repeating it for the second four counts. Sometimes, the dancers even dropped to the floor and added other similar antics. Many of the Tush Push variations were also written down and encouraged during instruction periods; others were carefully choreographed; while many others were just individually improvised on the dance floor.

Despite the published descriptions, there were many regional variations of the dances. Those variations included different names for similar song titles as well as vastly different step patterns to both songs and dances of the same names in other regions. Dygdon and Conger offered an explanation, "This 'regionalism' is part of the fun of Country & Western dancing. When we travel through the United States, we often find people doing a dance that looks familiar, but with some different steps" (3). They compared it to traveling around America and hearing people speak with "different regional dialects" (3). A few of the regional name differences with the same basic steps included,

Trashy Women and Horsin' Around
Ski Bumpus and Black Velvet
Electric Horseman and Bartender's Stomp
Cowboy Boogie and Charleston Rock
Cowboy Charleston and Charleston Cha Cha

Others had the same names, but were vastly different. In the case of the extremely popular Boot Scootin' Boogie, however, the dance had as many as 14 or 15 regional variations.

Boot Scootin' Boogie and Country Music Dance Remixes

"Boot Scootin' Boogie" was the fourth single released off the debut album *Brand New Man* by Brooks & Dunn's. In fact, Ronnie Dunn had actually written the song in 1989, a few years before he even teamed with Kix Brooks. For the song, Dunn told the story of an actual honky-tonk outside of Tulsa, Oklahoma, that he had frequented. The song lyrics perfectly captured the honky-tonk atmosphere, including the music, drinking, dancing, and relationships. Quite typical of many honky-tonks, Dunn's musical tale is of one located just outside the city limits. He also told of the patrons seeking relief from a hard day of work and simply having a good time as He also told of the patrons seeking relief from a hard day of work and simply having a good time on a crowded dance floor. The music added an upbeat danceable tempo to the lyrics that were soon recorded by the group Asleep at the Wheel, who achieved mild success with the song.

When Brooks & Dunn joined together as a duo and signed with the Arista Nashville record label in 1991, they included their version of "Boot Scootin' Boogie" on their debut album, *Brand New Man.* However, it was not immediately released as a single. Three other songs were released before it, with each gaining a #1 slot on the country music charts. Their debut song, "Brand New Man," quickly sold 250,000 singles. They followed with another up-tempo song, "My Next Broken Heart," and the hauntingly seductive, "Neon Moon." All the tracks were quite danceable and the first three singles contributed to mounting album sales, prompting the release of more songs from the album.

In similar fashion, when "Boot Scootin' Boogie" was released in the summer of 1992 as the duo's fourth single it quickly climbed to #1 on the *Billboard* country charts and remained at the top for four weeks. But in fact, prior to its radio release, many honky-tonk DJ's had been playing "Boot Scootin' Boogie" since the album's release months before. Within the dance halls and honky-tonks, the song was a dance floor favorite, routinely played night after night. All told, "Boot Scootin' Boogie" was a "monster" radio hit, and added to the line dance fervor. Unlike the Achy Breaky that had a standard dance, there were many different choreographed line dance versions for the song nationwide. In the case of Boot Scootin' Boogie, however, the dance had as many as 14 or 15 regional variations. And those were just the published versions. Yet, with the overwhelming success, a new breed of country music song was developed as a "dance mix" version of the song was released the following year.

At the time that *Brand New Man* was climbing the charts, Scott Hendricks, who co-produced Brooks & Dunn, brought up the idea of making a country dance mix. At first, he did not have any particular song in mind. As he recalled, "I was looking for someone to let me experiment creatively with their music, and 'Boot Scootin' Boogie' was a good candidate." In fact, some Arista Nashville execs were strongly opposed to any sort of Country music dance mix. Eventually producer Tim DuBois, who was unsure if any dance mix was right for country music, gave the go-ahead. But, the final decision was left to songwriter Ronnie Dunn and partner Kix Brooks who approved the project. According to DuBois, "To their credit, Kix and Ronnie said, 'Go for it.' A lot of people wouldn't have gone out on that limb." For the project, Hendricks enlisted a transplanted Los Angeles sound engineer named Brian Tankersley to put together the remix.

The sudden ascendancy of line dancing, however, did not sit well with hardcore country music fans; nor were they overly enthusiastic about the changing tempos of the music catering to danceable beats. All told, the idea of a studio-produced country dance mix of any song was quite radical. But, "Boot Scootin' Boogie" broke from tradition. As a radio single it clocked in at 3 minutes and 16 seconds; the dance mix on the other hand was extended to 6 minutes and 30 seconds. It was sent along to club DJs and also included on Brooks & Dunn's second album, *Hard Workin' Man*. The remix was titled "Boot Scootin' Boogie (Club Mix)." For unknown reasons, however, "Achy Breaky Heart" was soon relegated to novelty status, whereas "Boot Scootin' Boogie" remained a massive crowd favorite well into the 21st century. Many a working country bar band covered the song with positive audience response. While on the other hand, after 1994 or so, "Achy Breaky Heart" was rarely covered by a live band nor played by a DJ.

In 2003, Clarence Spalding, who co-managed Brooks & Dunn, recalled, "I've gone with other acts into places like Billy Bob's and, to this day, just as soon as that song comes on, people swarm the dance floor." In response to the staying power of "Boot Scootin' Boogie" as a dance floor favorite, Spalding simply added, "It was the right song at the right time." Nashville Arista Records producer Tim DuBois humorously added, "That [remix] started a revolution that a lot of us might have been better off without." In retrospect in 2003, Scott Hendricks, with a laugh, reluctantly admitted, "I'm not gonna say I thought it was a great idea, but it was the perfect song to do it with. And it started a phenomenon." The remix of "Boot Scootin' Boogie" certainly triggered a phenomenon, ushering in a slew of country music dance mixes. All told, the reason was simple; the title of a *Billboard* article in 2003 said it all, "The Remix of "Boot Scootin' Boogie" Got Fans Lining Up On Dance Floors across the Country" (Waddell, 1).

In a short time, there were thousands of new dances choreographed, as new hit songs and dance mixes appeared on the Country music charts. In reality, the Country music industry in Nashville was very much aware of the national trend not only for traditional country dancing and line dancing, but also that fans were buying up the music at record rates. During the mid-1990s, Country music was the largest selling genre of music in America, supplanting Rock and Hip Hop. The demand for danceable country music also led to a series of artists such as Scooter Lee, Kimber Clayton, and others who recorded music CDs specifically for the dance clubs. Songs such as Lee's very popular "Honky Tonk Twist," and Clayton's "Jose Cuervo" were soon standard across America and Europe. Due to songs such as Lee's and Clayton's, throughout the 1990s, the line dances became much more intricate than the earlier disco-era line dances and the Electric Slide. The country line dances varied from slow to fast paced, incorporating turns, kicks, hip swivels, syncopations, and also varied with rhythm styles including cha cha, waltz, East Coast Swing, West Coast Swing, and Two Step. (In later years, they even incorporated hip-hop, disco, Rock 'n' Roll, and Top-40 dance hits.)

Throughout the 1970s and into the 1980s, dance mixes were mainly associated with disco and freestyle dance clubs as well as DJ-catered affairs. In December 1992, however, the *USA Today* noted, "Special remixes for country dance clubs are common." Just about every artist had dance remixes of their hit country songs such as Mary Chapin Carpenter's "Down at the Twist and Shout" and Chris LeDoux's "Cadillac Ranch." LeDoux's song was also promoted in conjunction with a search for an original line dance to accompany the song named the LeDoux Shuffle. Even hard-core traditional country artists such as the honky-tonker Mark Chesnutt had their songs remixed for the dance floor. Some of Chesnutt's hits that were remixed included "Going to the Big D (And I Don't Mean Dallas)," "It's a Little Too Late," "Bubba Shot the Jukebox," and "Vicky Vance Just Wants to Dance." The Bellamy Brothers were one example that released an entire album of dance remixes of only their own music. They released *Dancin'*, featuring 11 re-mastered extended dance mixes of their past hit songs ("Music Swings toward Foot-Stomping Beats," 5D).

The popularity and demand prompted the release of full compilation albums of extended dance remixes. One of the first full-length compilations was *Country Dance Mixes* distributed by Atlantic

Records; it contained four cuts by Ray Kennedy who engineered and mixed the album. Two other extended mixes on *Country Dance Mixes* of "Trashy Women" by Confederate Railroad and "Life's a Dance" by John Michael Montgomery were very well received nationwide by country dancers, and became almost standard dance fare every night throughout the decade of the 1990s. Other dance mix compilations included, *The Most Awesome Line Dancing Album* (MFP Music 1997); *Country Dance Party* (K-Tel 1993); and *Bonanza Dance Party* (ZYK-Music) featuring "Cotton Eye Joe" by Rednex and "Swamp Thing" by The Grid. Both were techno dance mixes that did not sound very much like country music, but they were massive hits among the country line dancers. A compilation compact disc titled *Line Dance Fever* released in 1996 by Curb Music Company from London, England, also proved quite popular in the United States. The following year, *Line Dance Fever 2*, *Line Dance Fever* 3, and *Line Dance Fever* 4 were also released. In 1998, the demand continued with *Line Dance Fever 5*. Eventually the series of dance songs for line dancing extended to *Line Dance Fever 17* in 2008.

Partner Dances and Country Swing

Although the 1990s seemed dominated by country line dancing, the overall nationwide surge also created a renewed interest in many types of couple and partner dancing. A popular favorite was the standard Two Step from the 1980s Urban Cowboy era, with the addition of many more. By the 1990s, Country & Western dancing could easily be grouped into four types as, couple, partner, swing, and line. Couple dancing was the traditional lead-and-follow, including the Two Step, Waltz, Texas Polka, Triple Step, and variants such as the Houston Whip. Partner dancing was mainly the choreographed couple dances along the outside perimeter such as the 16-Step, Ten-Step, Blue Rose, Charleston Bump, Cowboy Cha Cha, El Paso, Kansas City Four Corners, Shadow, the Sidekick, and hundreds of others. Many of the partner dances had components of traditional lead and follow, but were performed in repeated sequences of choreographed moves similar to line dances. Some were performed face-to-face or side-by-side in positions, including the sweetheart, cape, and cuddle, among others.

Swing dances included the East Coast Swing and West Coast Swing. Some swing dances were choreographed in the same sequences as the partner dances, however, most incorporated many improvised moves reminiscent of the 1930s Jitterbug and 1950s Rock 'n' Roll. Actually, East Coast Swing (sometimes written as simply ECS) was the basic Jitterbug with the addition of triple steps in place of the single step, which was sometimes called Triple Swing and also resembled a version sometimes know as ballroom swing. East Coast Swing was danced in one spot mainly to medium tempo songs with a variety of underarm turns and, unlike the Jitterbug, a minimal amount of breakaways. As dancers partnered up for ECS and the like, some line dances were choreographed to match the songs such as "Company B," "Jive Boogie," "Jump Jive & Wail," "Miller Magic," "Miller Time," "Rock It," "Shorty George," "Swing City Jive," and "Zoot Suit Jive," among others.

As the trend in country line dancing continued, many dancers sought new experiences. Some experimented with other genres that benefited from the nationwide appeal of country dancing such as Cajun, Zydeco, and square dancing. Some of the basic Cajun dances were the Waltz, One Step, Two Step, and Jitterbug. Each of the dance steps closely resembled the basic steps of the social and ballroom versions of the dances; however, the Cajun style added a bit more bouncing and lively body movements in response to the music. Some others picked up on partner dances, such as West Coast Swing, that soon became standard in country dancing.

Slower tempo songs allowed the partners to do a dance called West Coast Swing. (sometimes WCS). It was characterized as a slot dance with a basic pattern known as the Sugar Push. The WCS might have well evolved in California from the Lindy Hop during World War II. Some credit the smooth Lindy Hop style of famed movie dancer Dean Collins that he adapted for small crowded dance floors as the forerunner of West Coast Swing. During the 1950s, however, California dance instructor Skippy Blair standardized the slotted West Coast Swing style. Since she was promoting that particular swing dance style on the west coast of America it was often called "Western Swing" to differentiate it from the basic swing dancing typically found around the rest of the country. But, as WCS became more popular, it was often confused with the western swing style of music that was so-named by Spade Cooley at about the same time. Therefore, in order to avoid confusion, by 1960 or so, Blair began calling it West Coast Swing. Sometimes the basic jitterbug style was called "eastern swing," which provides credibility for calling it East

Coast Swing on the Country & Western dance floors. Both the ECS and WCS are closely related to the Shag as danced in the Carolinas. The Shag can best be described as a hybrid of both ECS and WCS (Lichtmann, "West Coast Swing History").

Whereas the other swing dances could range in tempo from 120- to 170-beats per minute (bpm), West Coast Swing was usually performed at a much slower tempo in the 110- to 126-bpm ranges, and sometimes as slow as 80-bpm. Unlike the Hustle and other swing dances, which were danced around a "spot," the West Coast Swing was danced in a rectangular slot area about three feet wide and six feet long. The dance allowed for a myriad of dance moves. The woman also had the option to be playful and improvise, sometimes sultry, dance moves while traveling up and down within the "slot" as the man led her through as he casually stepped to the side and outside the slot. Although it was probably the most difficult rhythm to learn, it was also the most versatile. The West Coast Swing styles varied widely as did the places to dance. (Variations on the West Coast Swing included the Dallas Push, New Orleans Jamaica, and the Shag.) Unlike other dance styles it was not as widely known, but it did have a loyal following. It could be found in country-dance clubs all across America and was also danced to jazz, blues, pop, and disco.

By 2000, freestyle Cha Cha and other ballroom type dances such as Rumba, Salsa, and the Hustle also found their way into the Country & Western world. In an article for *The Washington Post*, journalist Kasper Zeuthen observed a similarity, but also a difference with the partner dancing. He described it as,

> In addition to line dancing, country and western dancing includes couples dancing, which is similar to standard ballroom dancing—with more yee-haws. Most couple dances derive from standards such as the fox trot and waltz. But rather than dancing to the strains of Johann Strauss, the dancers swirl to the likes of Brooks & Dunn. ("Suburban Cowboys," M23)

One regular, Bob Curran, who attended the monthly dance with his 13-year-old daughter, noted that unlike the formal atmosphere of ball-room, "Country dancing is a lot more relaxed" (Zeuthen, "Suburban Cowboys," M23).

Unlike other social dancing venues, it was possible for all four types of dancing to go on at the same time. In many cases it was not uncommon to see at least three types danced. An example would be a set partner dance such as the Sidekick on the perimeter, a line dance such as the CC Shuffle called for the inside, and an East Coast Swing on the corners. Sometimes an intrepid DJ would divide the line dances and call a different line dance for the front of the room and another for the back, while at the same time having a partner dance and swing dance going on. In that same manner it was also completely acceptable for a woman to ask a man to dance. Many clubs offered a slightly discreet method—buttons for women that stated, "Ask Me to Dance."

Country Dance Magazines and Line Dance Aerobics

In response to growing demand, many regional types of Country music and dance type of newsletters also arose. One national magazine was *Country Dance Lines*. In July 1984, the magazine had started with a mere eight pages, but by 1995, *Country Dance Lines* averaged over 110 pages. Many of those pages contained descriptions of dance steps and choreographed dances (mostly line dances). A monthly column listing titled, "Music for Dancing" provided a track-by-track listing of about 25 to 30 CDs each month. The track listings provided the beats per minute (bpm) and a suggested dance. Song titles in bold designated that the song had an especially strong dance beat. Each year *Country Dance Lines* also published a directory of instructors who taught country dancing. In 1998, the newsletter listed over 3,300 instructors in all 50 states and 16 foreign countries, including Australia, England, Canada, France, Germany, and even Saudi Arabia. In the year 2000, at the time that *Country Dance Lines* ceased publication, it included over 22,000 subscribers and had cataloged over 5,000 line and partner dances. During the mid-1990s, country line dancing was so popular in England that a magazine simply titled *Linedancer* was launched. It remained in monthly print publication until 2009 when it became Web-based.

Amidst it all, almost every major newspaper, magazine, or television station did a feature story on Country music and the line-dancing mania. They included, *The New York Times*, *USA Today*, *The Washington Post*, *The Boston Globe*, *New York Daily News*, *Los Angeles Times*, *The Austin Chronicle*, *Houston Chronicle*, the *Staten Island Advance*, *The Oregonian*, (Florida) *Citrus Times*, and *The St. Petersburg Times*, to name but a very

few. For those few newspapers that might not have assigned a columnist to visit directly, many others carried stories provided by corre-
spondents from news sources such as *The Associated Press*. Magazines
as diverse as *Time, Esquire, Billboard, The Christian Science Monitor,
American Fitness*, and *Texas Monthly*, once again to name but a very few,
also published stories. In reality, just about every (if not every) newspaper, magazine, and media outlet in America carried a feature story
on Country music and line dancing. In 1997, for example, M. S. Mason
surveyed the "country line dancing" scene in Denver, Colorado for
the stoic *Christian Science Monitor*. Mason noted that "Country-
western line dancing takes place in churches, social halls, and clubs
with names like Stampede, Country Palace, or the Grizzly Rose." (The
Grizzly Rose in Denver, Colorado, was still open by 2010.) To Mason's
surprise the music and dancing was described as "lively, sometimes
funny, and always a kick" (Mason, "Country Line Dancing," 78).

Health magazines such as *American Fitness* advertised the aerobic
capabilities of country line dancing. From YMCAs in New York City
on the east coast to the Parkside Athletic Club in Gilroy, California on
the west coast, just about every health and fitness club offered "Country Aerobics," or, more appropriately, providing aerobic classes to
country music. Kathy Fortmann noted,

> You don't have to go to a cowboy bar for line dancing or two-stepping.
> Country dancing is surging in popularity in health clubs. Propelled by
> the success of country dancing in nightclubs and contemporary, upbeat
> tunes, the latest choreography has a country-flavor. Different from funk
> which derived from techno music a few years ago, country moves can
> be easily mastered by participants of all fitness levels.

Typically participants signed up in eight-week segments for country
line dance orientated aerobics. Some, such as instructor Barbara Towe
at Parkside Athletic Club, accentuated their aerobics attire with "boots
and a bandanna." Similar to the lessons at the actual Country &
Western clubs, the aerobics classes started with basic moves such as
vine steps and each week added more complex moves and turns.
The aerobics classes, however, were not as structured as the line dancing clubs. Therefore, the instructors improvised on the choreography,
adding standard aerobic style moves, but the draw was the country
music and the line dancing appeal. Entrepreneurs looking to capitalize
on the phase, such as Power Productions and Dynamix, manufactured

various speed country tapes with a continuous bpm and solid eight-beat count (Fortmann, "Line 'em up!" 64–65).

Thousands of Places to Country Dance

For those who wanted the real experience of a country dance hall, by the mid-1990s, there were thousands of venues all across America that offered country dancing. Some were long established, including such Texas dance halls as Kendalia Halle, Anhalt, Twin Sisters, Luckenbach, and Gruene Hall, to name but a very few. At the time, many others opened all across the United States in hopes of capitalizing on the nationwide demand. New Jersey, as one example, had over 30 country dance clubs including the Colorado Cafe in Watchung, Dance 'n Style in Rockaway, the El Paso in Sayreville, Let's Dance Again in Hibernia, Prospectors in Cherry Hill, the Rocking Horse in Belleville, Oakley's in Princeton, the Yellow Rose in Manville, and the Whiskey Cafe in Lyndhurst. At that time, the Yellow Rose was listed by *Country American* magazine as the fourth most popular country dance club in America. By 2000, however, most had closed due to the fading desire among Americans to continue with country dancing. Both the Colorado Cafe and the Whiskey Cafe, however, were still in operation by 2010. Although in the case of the Whiskey Cafe, as was typical for many of those throughout America that had survived, the club often limited the country music dance nights to one-night a week and eliminated the live bands (Swarden, "Whooping and Hollering," NJ8).

In Charleston, South Carolina, Desperados had one of the largest music and entertainment clubs in the country. The country dance floor alone measured over 3,700 square feet and was capable of holding over 1,500 dancers. The perimeter bar and seating area was just as large, with an adjacent sports bar, catering hall, and a pool table area. Nearby in Greenville was the Blind Horse Saloon with a capacity of 1,200. A random sampling of other places to country dance across the United States included Desperado's Nightclub and Do Da's American Country in Fort Lauderdale, Florida; Brandin' Iron in San Bernardino, California; the Cadillac Ranch in Hartford, Connecticut; Boot Hill in Rapid City, South Dakota; and the Mishnock Barn in West Kingston, Rhode Island. The Mishnock Barn had three separate dance floors situated at different levels for partner, line-dance, and couples.

Between 1991 and 1993, in the Washington, D.C. area over 20 new country dance clubs joined some older ones. *Country Plus* magazine listed Country Junction in Rockville, Maryland; Latella's in Jessup; Murphy's Country Place in Rosedale; Lucas McCain's Saloon, in Frederick; Nashville's at the Timonium Holiday Inn; and Randy's California Inn between Baltimore and Washington. In Virginia, clubs featuring country dance included GW's and ZED, both in Alexandria, and the Red Moon Saloon at the Fair Oaks Mall. Within Washington, D.C., they had names such as Remington's at 639 Pennsylvania Avenue and Wild Oats located at 539 Eighth Street SE (Brenner, "Country Western Civilization," N7).

Country Junction in Rockville, Maryland, was over 20,000 square feet with two dance floors, three bars, a sit-down dining area, and a game room complete with pool tables and dartboards. The country dance floor often had over 600 people dancing to live country music bands. Within the club was a separate room with a 1,200 square foot dance floor. That area was for non-country dancing including swing most nights with the Hustle dance and disco on Saturdays. Adjacent to one of the smaller bars were about 12 small dining tables where patrons could order diner and listen to a live swing band. Eric Brace of *The Washington Post* described it as, "We've gone from 'Urban Cowboy' to 'Saturday Night Fever' in about 10 yards" (Brace, "Shake Your Cowboy Booties," N13).

In Arizona, Phoenix had two franchises of the Denim & Diamonds chain and also Mr. Lucky's, which operated as part of the Midnight Rodeo chain of Country & Western clubs home-based in Texas. The Mr. Lucky's in Phoenix had two floors of live entertainment and offered patrons both Country & Western and popular Top-40 dance music. The country music floor featured dancing with bands five nights of the week and DJ music between sets. Midnight Rodeo also owned country dance clubs in Amarillo, Lubbock, San Antonio, and Houston, all in Texas. A brief sampling in Texas included Wild West in Houston and Billy Bob's in Dallas. San Antonio had the Dallas club, Graham Central Station, and Cowboy's, among others. Other chains, such as those operated by Roger Gearhart, who owned eight in the Southwest, included Graham's in Oklahoma City, Cactus Moon in Abilene, Texas, and another Graham Central Station in Phoenix. Although Gearhart had eight in operation, he speculated, "I'm definitely seeing an increase in the number of country clubs in every market we're in" (Holley, "Country Dancing Sparks Club Growth," 1).

New York City and Denim & Diamonds

An unlikely market for country music and dancing was New York City. But the city had expanded beyond the country music bars of the Lone Star Café and Rodeo Bar that had maintained the country music tradition since the 1980s. Two popular country dance clubs that opened in New York City included the Pony Express in Staten Island and Denim & Diamonds in Manhattan. The Pony Express was cavernous, with a dance floor in excess of 3,000 square feet, and was often packed seven nights of the week with thousands of dancers. The club also featured live bands on occasion, ranging from Nashville recording stars such as Confederate Railroad, Darin Norwood, Scooter Lee, to local up-and-coming country bands including The Nashville Attitude.

Denim & Diamonds located in the heart of Manhattan at 48th Street and Lexington Avenue was a bit smaller, but also featured top country music acts including Chris LeDoux. Denim & Diamonds, which advertised itself as, "A Shot of Country With a Splash of Rock 'n' Roll," was a franchise with locations in New York, Los Angeles, Kansas City, Phoenix, and Santa Monica. In California, a Denim & Diamonds franchise had opened in Sacramento, in March 1991, and two others early the following year in Santa Monica and in Huntington Beach, among others. The franchise offered standard music and line dances, some unique only to their clubs. They even offered a range of merchandising including T-shirts, drinking glasses, denim jackets, and music CD's, such as *Favorite Line Dances as featured at Denim & Diamonds*, published by Scotti Bros. Records and distributed by BMG music in 1994 (Holley, "Country Dancing Sparks Club Growth," 1).

Denim & Diamonds was not the only place in Los Angeles for country dancing. Other Los Angeles area Country music clubs included the Palomino, the Longhorn Saloon, the Crazy Horse Saloon, and In Cahoots. Author Eve Babitz, in researching *Two by Two: Tango, Two-Step and the L.A. Night* (1999), frequented In Cahoots in Glendale, California. In comparing other dance styles and music, she noted a major distinction among men within the country dancing world. She observed, "All they have to be is a so-so two-step dancer, and they'll at least have American women asking them to dance" (44). But by 1999, In Cahoots was also closed. Babitz reasoned, "probably because dancers don't eat anything, don't drink anything but water, and don't want to spend any money" (44–45).

The New York chain of Denim & Diamonds opened in the heart of midtown Manhattan in March 1993 offering country dancing and lessons seven nights of the week. Operating out of a former disco dance club, the Manhattan location revamped entirely with western and cowboy paraphernalia. In deference to the disco era, a distinctive feature was a rotating mirrored saddle located above at the center of the dance floor. The New York City Denim & Diamonds held about 600 people, but could not accommodate all of them at one time on the dance floor. Therefore, an alternating format of twenty minutes of various line dancing and twenty minutes of Two Step and partner dancing was instituted. Often times the Denim & Diamonds DJ strung together a mix of two or three Two Step songs without stopping. That was usually followed by set choreographed partner dances such as the El Paso, Cowboy Cha Cha, and the Horseshoe, among others. Later in the evening, as non-country onlookers gathered, they added a 20-minute freestyle segment so all could dance. Only at off times, usually during the week and if the floor was relatively empty, would you find a mix of dance types on the floor at Denim & Diamonds. The smaller and often crowded dance floor, however, did not deter beginners, as the midtown Manhattan country dance club installed a small practice dance floor on a lower level. On the upper street level there was a bar that offered live Country music.

Country was quite popular in New York City, and that was not lost upon the media. All the major New York television news channels, such as *Good Day New York*, and daily newspapers including *The New York Times* had many feature stories. In August 1996, for example, *The New York Daily News* assigned journalist Michael O'Regan to write a story on Denim & Diamonds. Among the country dance lovers, he discovered an architect, a pattern designer, and a fashion model who counted themselves among some of the regulars that attended two or three times per week. Among his observations, he noted,

> New York City will never be mistaken for the wide-open plains of Texas or the Big Sky country of Montana, but even in the Big Apple you can find a place to do the Tush Push, the Boot Scootin' Boogie, or the Watermelon Crawl. Every night thousands of urban cowboys and cowgirls trade in their business suits and briefcases for a pair of old jeans and a

10-gallon hat to stomp the hours away at the few Wild West outposts scattered throughout the area. . . . And while they might be buried deep amid the concrete and skyscrapers, they manage to retain their western flavor with the help of props, décor and a good dose of old-fashioned country comfort." ("They Put the NY into Country," SP 16)

Unlike, the often oppressive atmosphere of many other New York City discos and dance clubs, many New Yorkers felt very comfortable at Denim & Diamonds. Among the Denim & Diamonds regulars was Susan Wyatt, a model for the Ford agency. For individuals such as herself and other fashion models, the country dance scene in Manhattan was without comparison. She said "clubs like Denim & Diamonds are a blessing for women who want to have fun without the hassle of men trying to pick them up. . . . We know we can just relax and enjoy ourselves here without being hit on all the time." Another regular added, "It's not like in a disco. People come here to dance, so it's a social, comfortable thing. There's no pressure" (O'Regan, SP 16).

At the time, it also seemed that just about any charity event, school function, festival, county fair, or fundraiser advertised a country line dance theme. In addition, there was an abundance of country dance themed weekends and festivals all over America. The weekends usually included a set price for a hotel room, dance instruction, work-shops, and nightly open dancing. In 1997, for example, a sampling listed in *Country Dance Lines* magazine of weekend events numbered over 100 in every state across America. Some of the events combined amateur dancing with professional dance competitions sanctioned by the United Country Western Dance Council (UCWDC). The UCWDC listed various country dance categories, such as professional, amateur, and age divisions. The dance competitors, and for that matter many of the amateur dancers, became overly conscious of their footwear. Many of the aficionados who had taken to wearing authentic cowboy boots realized that they were heavy and not all that comfortable for dancing. As a result, they sought out shoes made specifically for dancing. Some purchased ballroom shoes such as Diamante, Tic Tac Toe, and Leo's Giordano. However, one company, Evenin' Star Pro Dance Boots manufactured footwear that looked very much like cowboy boots but was specially designed for dancing. A distinctive feature was a "doubled cushioned chrome leather sole," and they were about one-third the weight.

Evenin' Star Pro Dance Boots manufactured footwear that looked very much like cowboy boots, but were specially designed for dancing. This 1998 ad appeared in *Country Dance Lines* magazine October/November Vol. 28, nos. 4 and 5, p. 2. (Used by Permission of Dancin' Cowboy, Inc., Courtesy of Steve Clarkson.)

Line Dancing Spreads from Country to Country

By 1995, the line dancing craze spread overseas to Europe. At the same time, most of the dances were from America and also matched to Country & Western music. In Europe, however, the main appeal was mostly for line dancing only. The pattern of instruction in countries such as England, Norway, Denmark, France, and others, was also very similar to that in the United States. In 1996, Americans Judy Dygdon and Tony Conger published an instruction book in England, *Country & Western Line Dancing: Step-by-Step Instructions for Cowgirls & Cowboys.* They offered up a bit of history to the Brits by proudly boasting, "Line Dancing began in the USA" (iii).

Although the country line dance style of the mid-1990s was distinctly American, it could easily have been argued that the development of English country dancing in the 16th century John Playford style and resurrected by Cecil Sharpe in the early 20th century was the original. In fact, Americans, combined with their European ancestors, had danced in contra lines for many centuries. But, the emergence of line dancing especially in connection with Country music during the 1990s, was something very different. In that same sense, although square dancing and many folk dance styles that emerged after World War II were connected to Country & Western music, it was also not the same as the 1990s partner or line dancing. In some cases, some of the line dancing that grew from the country line dance world found its way into many of the square, folk, ballroom, and social dance worlds.

Nevertheless, it was the combination of Country music and line dancing that attracted Europeans. To make the instruction book complete, the publishers, Sigma Press in Cheshire, England, added a music CD for the accompanying line dances. The songs were cover versions performed by a studio group named The Rustler's and recorded at Sound & Fury Productions and Mast Audio in the New York and New Jersey area. In trying to explain the appeal of line dancing, either within America or even in Europe, Dygdon and Conger surmised,

> Perhaps Country and Western dancing appeals to many because of the music to which it is danced. Perhaps it is popular because Country and Western dancing has now become more professional: you can take

lessons in it and there are competitions for dancers and choreographers. Many people enjoy Country and Western dancing because you can dance even if you don't have a partner. Whatever the reasons for the trend, Country and Western dancing was not born with the trend, and it will not die when the trend has run its course. (4)

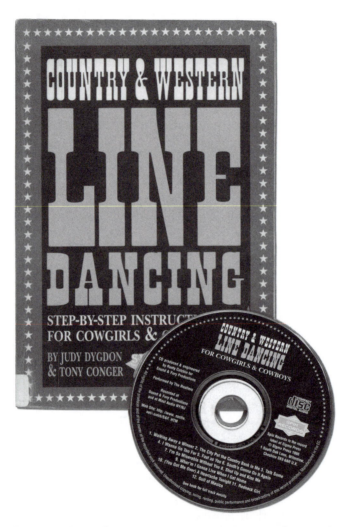

This 1996 instruction book *Country & Western Line Dancing: Step-by-Step Instructions for Cowgirls & Cowboys* was published in England. Author's Judy Dygdon and Tony Conger, both Americans, offered up a bit of history to the British by proudly boasting, "Line Dancing began in the USA." To make the instruction book complete, a music CD was included. (Used by permission of Sigma Press. Courtesy of Graham Beech.)

The End of the Country Line Dance Fad

Both the country music dance clubs and line dance instructors tried to keep up with the ever-growing list of new dances. But it did require constant attention and updating on a regular basis. That regularity for some was at least once a week, and for others it was literally seven nights a week. Many die-hards met the challenge, but to that same end also would complain if during a four- or five-hour evening even one of the line dances were repeated. Therefore, during the course of an evening, it was not unusual for a DJ to be under pressure to produce songs for 65 to 70 different dances. A very good DJ would try to appease the line dancers, couples, and swing dancers, and therefore that number could easily double or triple. In the same manner, if a DJ or a band called out just a couple's dance, many of the "line dance only" group would literally assault the DJ booth or complain to the band for specific songs only for line dancing.

The complaints from "purists" were twofold. Some had ardently listened to Country music and danced to it prior to the national fad and even before the *Urban Cowboy* craze. Other so-called "purists" were in essence those who came into the country dance world around 1991 and 1992, when just about everything played was a country song. Many of them were also completely unaware of line dancing history prior to country songs such as "Achy Breaky Heart." As the country line dance craze was spreading nationwide, many of the newer participants enjoyed learning dances such as Copperhead Road, Cruisin', and Mustang Sally. But, in fact, each of those, as well as quite a few others, had line dancing roots in the 1980s and were non-country. Copperhead Road was danced to the song of the same name by Steve Earle; Cruisin' was often wedded to "Still Cruisin" by the Beach Boys; and Mustang Sally went with the song of the same name by Wilson Pickett or The Commitments. Each of these were distinctly non-country and were basically rock, pop, and rhythm & blues, respectively (Powell, "What Is Line dancing?").

Actually within the country dance venues, not everyone was a fan of Country music, but all were there for the dancing. As a result, there was also an adaptation of the music applied to line dancing. In a short time, professional dance instructors looked beyond Country music for songs of interest to appeal to a diverse group of individuals who enjoyed line dancing, but were not necessarily concerned over the strictly Country music format. Therefore, as huge worldwide pop hits such as Gina G's "Oh Eh Just a Little Bit," and Ricky Martin's "Living La Vida Loca" hit the airwaves, the line dance choreographers adapted them to line dancing. Quite a few, including the two mentioned, were often played in the country dance halls.

In addition, the line dance only crowd was attracted to weekend events that catered to introducing sometimes 50 or so new line dances. In turn, many of those songs were choreographed to non-country songs such as "Stray Cat Strut" by the Stray Cats, "Strokin" by Clarence Carter, "Swing to the Mood," by the Jive Bunny's, and electronic dance mixes such as "Ooh Eeh" by Gina G. and "Swamp Thang." A tiff developed between those who wanted only country music—mostly Two-stepping country couples—and those who wanted the non-country line dances. A term that was often applied by some DJs and bands to those individuals was "Line Dance Nazi's."

Nevertheless, the challenge to keep up with the onslaught was overwhelming to many. In a short time, even attending a music club once-a-week was not enough. For those that attended every two weeks, it appeared that what they had learned in the last month was not even played or called anymore. For many onlookers who attended, most often out of curiosity, but also with the hope of joining in the fun, it was overwhelming to even begin to learn even a few basic dances. In essence it took a lot of work and even studying the steps from pre-printed step sheets to keep current. That was, in all likelihood, why the line dance craze came to a sudden end around 1997.

In essence, when a "fun" leisure activity becomes work, it is no longer fun. The other attachment was that, as the line dance craze grew, so did the amount of venues offering country music. But in order to support the cost of operating large venues, clubs relied on heavy alcohol sales. In the case of the "newbies" to country dancing, many did not drink in a capacity to provide a monetary profit. Therefore, a combination of the two led to the sudden end of line dancing. In rapid succession, many of the Country music dance clubs disappeared almost as quickly as they had appeared a few years earlier.

Conclusion

Country Dancing
and the Future

"Real country dancing never seems to change."
—Patsy Swayze, choreographer

At the beginning of the 21st century, many of the century-old country dance halls were still going strong, as were a few that had opened during the line dance fad of the 1990s. For the most part, however, many of the country dance venues such as the Denim & Diamonds chain in the big cities of New York, Los Angeles, Detroit, and Phoenix had long since closed. So had many others that had opened during the country line dance mania of the 1990s. On the other hand, for that matter, most of them never really maintained a tradition of dancing to Country & Western music—they simply jumped on the fad as it came and went. In an assessment of country dancing in general, Patsy Swayze, who choreographed the 1980 movie *Urban Cowboy*, offered an observation. She said, "real country dancing never seems to change. It always seems to go on and on, maybe bigger and better depending on how hot the music is" (Zimmerman, 5D).

By the year 2000 and into 2010, country dancing did not disappear as much as it just was no longer a nationwide fad. Many of the old traditional mainstays remained—most of them continuing in the tradition of the basic Two Step, Waltz, Swing, and other partner dances. Also, small segments of hardcore line dancing devotees continued on, although in much smaller numbers than during the height of the 1990s.

Many of the dance halls cut back on their schedules of country line dancing, often to only one or two nights a week. In southern Indiana, Mike's Music & Dance Barn located on Highway 46 about four miles west of Nashville and twelve miles from Bloomington was one example. The club posted a weekly schedule of various events. Sunday offered karaoke from 6:00 to 10:00 P.M. Mondays and Thursdays continued with country line dance lessons. Fridays were a mixed bag of dance events. The first and third Friday of the month sponsored a "singles dance." The second Friday of each month featured a "Ballroom Night."

Although ballroom lessons were taught, a "smooth country band" played country music suitable for the Waltz, Cha Cha, Rumba, and others. In an age-old tradition, Saturday nights were still Country

By 2010, many of the country dance halls cut back on their weekly schedules. In southern Indiana, Mike's Music & Dance Barn was one example that posted a weekly schedule of various dance events. On Saturday nights, however, they still retained the age-old tradition of live Country music and dancing. (Photographs by Frank Rogoyski and used by permission of Mike's Music and Dance Barn)

music and country dancing. A house band played live Country music from 8:00 to 11:00 P.M. Usually the dance floor was filled (http://www.TheDanceBarn.com/schedule.php).

Some others, such as Club 412 in New York City, advertised country dances only on special occasions. The announcements were made much easier by the technology offered by the World Wide Web and the Internet. Line dancing was often embraced among the gay and lesbian community. In 2009, Dance Manhattan Studios in New York City, for example, advertised the "Big Apple Ranch," which was a line dancing party for the gay community. The cowboy image and line dancing was also featured in an episode from the Logo cable television show *Adam and Steve*. Known as the "Gay cowboy dance scene," it was an extremely popular YouTube hit in 2008/2009.

By 2010, many of the country dance halls still served up nightly doses of music and dancing. Some, such as Twin Sisters Dance Hall, built by German immigrants around 1880 in Texas, still sponsored dances on the first Saturday of the month. Another still in operation was Gruene Hall built in 1878. A much newer dance hall tradition was Graham Central Station in San Antonio, Texas. The cavernous mall-like dance club featured multiple dance clubs within one building for Tejano,

A much newer dance hall tradition was Graham Central Station in San Antonio, Texas. The cavernous mall-like dance club featured multiple dance clubs within one building for Tejano, Freestyle, House, Classic Rock, and Country music. (Author's Archives)

freestyle, house, Classic Rock, and Country music. Some other stalwarts included the Whiskey Cafe in Lyndhurst and the Colorado Cafe in Scotch Plains, both in New Jersey; the Cadillac Ranch in Hartford, Connecticut; Wild West in Houston; and the Grizzly Rose in Denver, Colorado, among many hundreds of others. Quite a few of them also featured a mechanical bull reminiscent of the Urban Cowboy days.

Mickey Gilley also kept the old tradition alive, as he opened namesake clubs in Dallas and Las Vegas. The tradition of *Urban Cowboy* was also revived in a short-lived Broadway musical co-written by Aaron Latham and Phillip Oesterman. It played in previews from November 5 to December 1, 2002, in Florida's Coconut Grove Playhouse and later opened on Broadway in New York City at the Broadhurst Theater on March 27, 2003. The play, however, was not a hit, closing quickly on May 18, 2003, after a total of 26 previews and only 60 regular performances. During the fall of 2004, however, the stage version of *Urban Cowboy* was launched on a nationwide tour of college campuses and smaller playhouses to generally good response.

Although written in 1995, a statement in an article for *Texas Monthly* by John Morthland could have easily applied to 2010. He said, "real country dancing never went away, and many old community dance halls thrive amid the glitzy newcomers." Many of those still offered dancing, but the main draw was dancing to live Country music. Some others did not generally object to the dancing, but only if it was with Country music in the honky-tonk tradition. One example was the Broken Spoke in Austin, Texas, that had first opened in 1964. Michael Corcoran properly clarified the atmosphere in an online article for *Austin360.com*. He explained, "The Broken Spoke is a boot-slidin' paradise, haunted by the ghosts of true country music, but don't call it a dancehall. . . . the Spoke is a honky-tonk" ("Come Dancing").

Country singer Pat Green, himself born in Texas, was a fan of playing in the age-old dance halls and honky-tonks throughout his home state. He equated his feeling of playing in those legendary halls as a youngster with aspirations of playing baseball and "stepping up to the plate at Yankee Stadium." Green was such a fan of the music and dance tradition that in 2008 he wrote a book on the history of the Texas dance halls called *Pat Green's Dance Halls & Dreamers*. He was not alone. In 2002, Geronimo Treviño provided an exhaustive list in *Dance Halls and Last Calls: A History of Texas Country Music*. In 2007, Gail Folkins also authored similar homage in *Texas Dance Halls: A Two-Step Circuit*. Each publication was heavily illustrated and provided wonderful anecdotes both current and reminiscent. In fact, all the publications echoed similar sentiments to Bill Porterfield's 1983 publication, *The Greatest Honky-Tonks in Texas*. A similar sentiment was that the old wooden floors could tell a history of Country & Western dance all in itself.

An apt description was noted by Michael Corcoran as the wooden dance floors were not anywhere near the polished perfection of a gymnasium floor. The standard dull sheen was the result of years and years of thousands of Two-steppers who provided what Corcoran called "sole-polished wooden floors." The dance halls did not have to be fancy. The main ingredient, as seen on the Silver Bullet Saloon located south of San Antonio in Texas simply advertised as, "Dance Hall." But, at the beginning of the 21st century as it was with the 1920s, or for that matter dating back to earlier traditions, the condition of a Country & Western dance floor did not matter. What did matter was having a space to dance and a Country music band playing dance-able music. And when the band started up the music, no one needed any prodding to get out on the floor and dance. In fact, the dancing was almost instinctively intertwined with the spirit of it all.

The Country music dance halls did not have to be fancy. The main ingredient, as seen on the Silver Bullet Saloon located south of San Antonio in Texas was "Dance Hall." (Used by permission of Thelma Lynn Olsen)

Bibliography

Books

Babitz, Eve. *Two by Two: Tango, Two-Step and the L.A. Night*. New York: Simon & Schuster, 1999.

Boyd, Jean A. *The Jazz of the Southwest: An Oral History of Western Swing*. Austin: University of Texas Press, 1998.

Brackenbury, Jan. *Kountry Kickers: Country Western Line Dance Manual*. Sun Prairie, WI: Wolf Creek Publishing, 1986.

Casey, Betty. *Dance Across Texas*. Austin: University of Texas Press, 1985.

Claypool, Bob. *Saturday Night at Gilley's*. New York: Delilah/Grove Press, 1980.

Driver, Ian. *A Century of Dance: A Hundred Years of Musical Movement, from Waltz to Hip Hop*. London: Octopus Publishing Group Limited, 2000.

Dygdon, Judy and Tony Conger. *Country & Western Line Dancing: Step-by-Step Instructions for Cowgirls & Cowboys*. Cheshire, England: Sigma Press, 1996.

Folkins, Gail. *Texas Dance Halls: A Two-Step Circuit*. Lubbock, TX: Texas Tech University Press, 2007.

Ginell, Cary. *Milton Brown and the Founding of Western Swing*. Chicago: University of Illinois Press, 1994.

Giordano, Ralph G. *Fun and Games in Twentieth Century America: A Historical Guide to Leisure*. Westport, CT: Greenwood, 2003.

———. *Satan in the Dance Hall: The Rev. John Roach Straton, Social Dancing, and Morality in 1920s New York City*. Lanham, MD: The Scarecrow Press, 2008.

———. *Social Dancing in America: Fair Terpsichore to the Ghost Dance 1607 to 1900*. Vol. 1. Westport, CT: Greenwood, 2006.

———. *Social Dancing in America: Lindy Hop to Hip Hop 1901 to 2000*. Vol. 2. Westport, CT: Greenwood, 2006.

Goodman, Benny and Irving Kolodin. *The Kingdom of Swing*. New York: Frederick Ungar Publishing Company, 1939 (reprint 1961).

Green, Pat, Luke Gilliam, and Gut Rogers. *Pat Green's Dance Halls & Dreamers*. Texas: University of Texas Press, 2008.

Halberstam, David. *The Fifties*. New York: Metro Books, 2001.

Harris, Jane A., Anne M. Pittmann, Marlys S. Waller, and Cathy L. Dark. *Dance a While: Handbook for Folk, Square, Contra, and Social Dance*. 8th ed. Boston: Allyn and Bacon, 2000.

Kraus, Richard. *Recreation and Leisure in Modern Society*. New York: Appleton-Century-Crofts, 1971.

Leisner, Tony. *The Official Guide to Country Dance Steps*. Secaucus, NJ: Chartwell Books, Inc., 1980.

Livingston, Peter. *The Complete Book of Country Swing & Western Dance and a Bit about Cowboys*. Garden City, NY: Livingston/Boulder Books, 1981.

Lustgarten, Karen. *The Complete Guide to Disco Dancing: The Easy Step-by-Step Way to Learn Today's Top Dances*. New York: Warner Books, 1978.

Miller, Craig. *Social Dance in the Mormon West*. Salt Lake City: The Utah Arts Council, 2000.

Needham, Maureen. "All Lined Up at the Wildhorse Saloon," in Maureen Needham, *I See America Dancing: Selected Readings 1685–2000*. Chicago: University of Illinois Press, 2002, 81–84. (Originally published as "Everybody Move!" in *The Nashville Scene*, September 18, 1997.)

Nevell, Richard. *A Time to Dance: American Country Dancing from Hornpipes to Hot Hash*. New York: St. Martin's Press, 1977.

Orlean, Susan. *Saturday Night*. New York: Knopf, 1990.

Porterfield, Bill. *The Greatest Honky-Tonks in Texas*. Dallas, TX: Taylor Publishing Company, 1983.

Rusher, Shirley and Patrick McMillan. *Kicker Dancin' Texas Style: How to Do the Top Ten Country-Western Dances*. Winston-Salem, NC: Hunter Textbooks Inc., 1988.

Shaw, Lloyd. *The Round Dance Book*. Caldwell, ID: Caxton Printers, Ltd., 1949.

Stuart, Nancy Rubin. *Club Dance Scrapbook: The Show, the Steps, the Spirit of Country*. Atlanta, GA: Lionheart Books, 1998.

Townsend, Charles R. *San Antonio Rose: The Life and Music of Bob Wills*. Chicago: University of Illinois Press, 1986.

Treviño III, Geronimo. *Dance Halls and Last Calls: A History of Texas Country Music*. Plano, TX: Republic of Texas Press, 2002.

Uslan, Michael and Bruce Solomon. *Dick Clark's the First 25 Years of Rock and Roll*. New York: Dell, 1981.

Woodroof, Nancy and Aubrey Woodroof. *The Big Book of Country Western Dancing*. Escondido, CA: NAP Productions, 1996.

Periodicals

———— "Acuff & the Grand Ole Opry." *Roughstock's History of Country Music*, http://www.roughstock.com/history/acuff.html.

Applebome, Peter. "Country Meets Disco in the 'Citified' West." *The New York Times*, August 29, 1979, C1.

Archer, Rick. "Disco Rises from the Ashes—Western Swing Is Born!" *SSQQ*, 1999 Chapter 5. http://www.ssqq.com/stories/westernswing5.htm.

————. "The Arrival of 'Urban Cowboy' Is Followed by Seeds of Discontent." *SSQQ*, 1999 Chapter 4, http://www.ssqq.com/stories/westernswing4.htm.

————. "The Beginnings," *Roughstock's History of Country Music*, http://www.roughstock.com/history/begin.html.

———. "Bill Monroe and Bluegrass," *Roughstock's History of Country Music*, http://www.roughstock.com/history/bgrass.html.

Boehlert, Eric. "Country Stations Step to the Line to Woo New Listeners." *Billboard*, March 27, 1993, 80.

Bourke, Brian G. "Two-Step Fever Country Western Dancing Receives Gentle Push Locally." *The Post-Standard*, January 16, 1992, Lifestyle, 1.

Brace, Eric. "Shake Your Cowboy Booties." *The Washington Post*, March 1, 1996, Weekend, N13.

———. *The Billboard NAMM Trade Show and Convention Section*. July 15, 1950.

Brenner, Joel Glenn. "Country Western Civilization." *The Washington Post*, October 29, 1993, Weekend, N7.

———. "Cain's Ballroom," *Tulsa Preservation Society Online*. http://tulsapreservation commission.org/nationalregister/buildings/index.pl?id=13.

Canby, Vincent. "Travolta, 'Urban Cowboy'." *The New York Times*, June 11, 1980, C21.

Carton, Barbara. "N. Va. Gets a Kick Out of Country; Boots Were Made for Dancing." *The Washington Post*, March 10, 1988, Metro, B1.

Chadwick, Susan. "The Two Step: It's a Simple Step. But Done to Tricky Country Rhythm, It's Texas' Most Dignified Dance." *TexasMonthly.com*, http://www.texasmonthly.com/ranch/readme/twostep.php.

Clevenger, Chris. "Couple Find Country Dancing in Their Hearts." *Citrus Times*, January 18, 1993, Monday, City Edition, 1.

Cohn, Nik. "Tribal Rites of the New Saturday Night." *New York Magazine*, June 7, 1976.

———. "Cowboy Music." *Roughstock's History of Country Music*, http://www.roughstock.com/history/cowboy.html.

Corcoran, Michael. "Country Dancehalls Preserve Texas History. Community and Tradition still Meet Up for Boot-Scootin' and Socializing." *Austin360.com*, February 12, 2008 (originally published December 9, 2007). http://www.austin 360.com/recreation/content/recreation/guides/visit/dancehall.html.

Crowley, Carolyn Hughes. "Ballroom Dancing, Cowboy-Style." *Christian Science Monitor*, November 24, 1989, Leisure, 14.

Demarest, Michael. "C & W Nightclubs: Riding High." *TIME*, February 2, 1981, http://www.time.com/time/magazine/article/0,9171,920982,00.html.

DeWitt, Dan. "Boot Scottin' Fun." *St. Petersburg Times*, March 22, 1993, 1.

Erlewine, Stephen Thomas. "Milton Brown, the Other King of Western Swing." *All-Music Guide*, http://elvispelvis.com/miltonbrown.htm.

Ford, Royal. "It's Not the Same Old Twang; New Rhythms, Rhymes Drawing New Englanders Back to Country Music." *The Boston Globe*, May 23, 1993, 40.

Fortmann, Kathy. "Line 'em up!" *American Fitness*, 11, no. 5, 64–65.

Fredricksen, Barbara L. "Country Dancing Steps Up Heart, Fun." *St. Petersburg Times*, July 16, 1994, City Edition, 1.

Friskics-Warren, Bill. "Eddy Arnold, 89, Country Singer with Pop Luster, Dies." *The New York Times*, May 9, 2008, C11.

Garcia, Guy, and Dan Cray. "Scoot Your Booty! Fed Up with Discos and Singles Bars, Urban Cowboys Are Lining Up for the Newest Dance Craze," *TIME*, March 15, 1993, http://www.time.com/time/magazine/article/0,9171,977982-1,00.html.

———. "Garth and New Country," *Roughstock's History of Country Music*, http://www.roughstock.com/history/garthnew.html.

Gray, Christopher. "The Mother of All Texas Honky-Tonks, *Live at Gilley's*." *The Austin Chronicle Online*, http://www.austinchronicle.com/gyrobase/Issue/story?oid=oid%3A74248.

Grimes, Amber. "In the Swing." *St. Petersburg Times*, February 10, 1992, City Edition, 1.

Hamill, Sean D. "A City Sees Its Past, and Maybe Future, in a Theater." *The New York Times*, March 6, 2009, A13.

Hatfield, Julie. "These Boots Are Made for Dancing; the Latest Dance Fad Spurs Sales of Western Wear." *The Boston Globe*, March 26, 1994, 25.

Holley, Debbie, "Country Dancing Sparks Club Growth; New Nightclubs, Remixes Target Trend." *Billboard*, June 6, 1992, 1.

———— "Houston Celebrates 'Urban Cowboy'." *Associated Press*, June 6, 1980, Friday, PM cycle.

Hynes, Warren. "Yeeee-Ha! It's Time to Get Off the Couch and into the Barn; Country Line Dancing Is Sweeping Staten Island." *Staten Island Advance*, June 5, 1995, B1.

————. "Having Fun Dancing." *Nebraska Living History Farm Project*, http://www.livinghistoryfarm.org/farminginthe30s/life_18.html.

Latham, Aaron. "The Ballad of the Urban Cowboy: America's Search for True Grit." *Esquire*, September 12, 1978.

Lichtmann, Kurt. "West Coast Swing History." *Cornell University*. http://ithacaswingdance.com/Link15wcs.html.

Lomax, III, John. "Country Music." *Microsoft Encarta® Encyclopedia 2000.*

Mansfield, Duncan. "Nashville Sound: Cable Show Has 'em Two-Steppin'." *Associated Press*, June 21, 1991, Friday, BC cycle.

————. "Last Dance at Popular Nashville TV Club." *Associated Press*, January 25, 1999. http://archive.southcoasttoday.com/daily/01-99/01-25-99/c01ae078.htm.

Mason, M. S. "Country Line Dancing." *Christian Science Monitor*, April 16, 1997, 78–79.

McNees, Pat. "Let's Shuffle, Pardner." *The Washington Post*, November 4, 1988, Weekend, N6.

Milligan, Heather. "Gilley's." *The Handbook of Texas Online*, http://www.tshaonline.org/handbook/online/articles/GG/xdg2.html.

Milloy, Courtland. "The Dance That Would Not Die." *The Washington Post*, October 3, 1989, B3.

Morthland, John. "Come Dancing." *Texas Monthly* 23, no. 3 (March 1995) 78–85.

————. "Music Swings Toward Foot-Stomping Beats." *USA TODAY*, December 1, 1992, 5D.

Navarro, Mireya. "Macarena Madness Takes the Floor." *The New York Times*, December 27, 1995, A10.

O'Regan, Michael. "They Put the NY into Country: An Architect, a Designer and a Model — are All Regulars at Manhattan's Top Country 'n' Western Club." *The New York Daily News*, August 25, 1996, SP 16–17.

Palmer, Robert. "Milton Brown and his Musical Brownies." *FI Magazine*, June 1997, http://thompsonian.info/palmer-review.html.

Patton, Phil. "Achy Breaky: A 22-Step Line-Dance Sensation with Billy Ray Cyrus's Cheatin'-Heart No. 1 Single." *The New York Times*, August 16, 1992, V8.

Paulson, Janet. "Clackamas County Fete to Include Tush Push." *The Oregonian*, March 3, 1994, 5.

Pfeffer, Murray L. "Western Swing Bands History." 1988–2006. http://info.net/usa/weswing.html#Hofner.

Powell, David. "What Is Line dancing?" *Silver Stetsons Online*, January 2003. http://www.silverstetsons.co.uk/other%20stuff/linedance%20history.htm.

Pugh, Clifford. "La Macarena; Dance and Song Bridge Cultural Gap." *The Houston Chronicle*, January 23, 1996, 1.

Sandow, Greg. "Grand Ole Opry." *Microsoft Encarta® Encyclopedia 2000*.

Schoemer, "A Pop Star Shining in the Glow of Success." *The New York Times*, July 1, 1992, C13.

Schwed, Mark. "Bucking Bull Mania Spreads; Thousands Pay to Get Thrown." *Associated Press United Press International*, October 12, 1980, Sunday, BC cycle.

Spilner, Maggie. "Country-Western 101." *Prevention*, March 1993.

Stevens, William K. "Cowboy Culture Yields, Even in the Heart of Texas, to Un-Chic Bunny Hop. *The New York Times*, April 19, 1982, A16.

Swarden Carlotta Gulvas. "Whooping and Hollering, It's Country-and-Western Dancing." *The New York Times*, April 17, 1994, NJ8.

Thompson, Bill. "Interview with Roy Lee Brown—Part 1 (recorded on April 18, 2004)." http://thompsonian.info/Roy-Lee-Brown-Interview-Part-1.html.

———. "Interview with Roy Lee Brown—Part 2 (recorded on April 18, 2004)." http://thompsonian.info/Roy-Lee-Brown-Interview-Part-2.html.

Townsend, Charles R. "Homecoming: Reflections on Bob Wills and His Texas Playboys, 1915–1973." *Southland Records.com*, http://www.southlandrecords.com/willsbob.htm

Turczyn, Coury. "Dance Fever: Way, Way Back When in the '90s, Line Dancing Became Not Only a National Craze, But a Way of Life." *Metro Pulse*, June 30, 1994, http://www.popcultmag.com/obsessions/fadsandphenoms/linedancing/linedance1.html.

Waddell, Ray. "The Remix of 'Boot Scootin' Boogie' Got Fans Lining Up on Dance Floors across the Country." *Billboard* 115, no. 25 (June 21, 2003): 1.

Walsh, Jeanne Cook. "Dancing Through the Depression." *Oldtime Nebraska*. http://www.olden-times.com/oldtimenebraska/n-jwalsh/dancers.html.

Watrous, Peter. "He's Hot and Not Just to Fans of Country." *The New York Times*, June 10, 1992, C15.

Weber, Joel R. "Disco Yields to Western Swing." *The New York Times*, October 25, 1981, Sunday, Section 11; Connecticut, 13.

———. "Western Swing Bands: A History." *Big Bands Database*. http://nfo.net/usa/weswing.html.

———. "Western Swing, the Beginnings." *Roughstock's History of Country Music*, http://www.roughstock.com/history/westernswing.html.

———. "Hank Williams." *Microsoft® Encarta® Encyclopedia 2000*. Microsoft Corp.

———. "Yee-Ha! Bar Has a Whiff of the West." *The New York Times*, April 21, 1993, B6.

Zeuthen, Kasper. "Suburban Cowboys." *The Washington Post*, February 10, 1999, Weekend, M23.

Zibart, Eve. "Jus' Do-si-do to the Junction." *The Washington Post*, August 26, 1988, Weekend, N19.

Zimmerman, David. "Chipman Hoofing It to Two-Step Stardom." *USA TODAY*, December 1, 1992, 5D.

———. "Country Dancing Keeps in Step with Modern Times." *USA TODAY*, December 1, 1992, 5D.

Video and DVD

Country Dancing Made Easy with Jerry Staeheli. Greg James Productions, 1993.
Footloose. Directed by Herbert Ross, Paramount Pictures, 1984, DVD Release, 2002.
Rock 'n' Roll Explodes. The History of Rock 'n' Roll Series. Videocassette. Directed by Andrew Solt. Time Life Video & Television and Warner Bros. 1995.
Urban Cowboy. Directed by James Bridges, Paramount Pictures, 1980, DVD Release 2002.

YouTube Videos

Club Dance (http://youtube.com/watch?v=ExBEihXOlA0&feature=related)

- Tush Push and ECS: song "Honky Tonk World," by Chris LeDoux.
- Two Step and Ski Bumpus: song "Living on Life No. 9," by Martina McBride.
- Schottische: song, "We Can Hold Our Own," by Ronna Reeves.

Club Dance (http://youtube.com/watch?v=aO0LvFpWDpY&feature=related)

- Tush Push: song "If I Could Make a Living Out of Loving You," also with Phil Campbell and Shelley Mangrum talking with artist Clay Walker.
- Triple-Step and 16-Step: song "I Don't Even Know Your Name," by Alan Jackson.

Instructional Video (http://youtube.com/watch?v=3xZdMfZD5l0&feature=related)

- Country Electric Slide with Brooke Dance.

Spade Cooley King of Western Swing. Warner Bros. Pictures, 1945. http://www.youtube.com/watch?v=CsiNkWYEXjE.

Record Albums

Ray Benson and Asleep at the Wheel, *Asleep at the Wheel's Ride With Bob!! A Tribute to Bob Wills and The Texas Playboys*. DRMD-50117. 1999 SKG Music Nashville LLC DreamWorks Records, Nashville.
Ray Benson and Asleep at the Wheel, *Asleep at the Wheel—Tribute to the music of Bob Wills and The Texas Playboys*. CDP-7243-8-28063-2-5. 1994 Liberty Records, Nashville.
Urban Cowboy. Soundtrack Album Compilation, Paramount Pictures Corp. 1980. Elektra/Asylum/Nonesuch Records, no. DP 90002.
Dancin'. Bellamy Brothers Records, distributed by Intersound Inc. Catalog no. 9186.

Documents

Milton Brown and the Musical Brownies Promotional Calendar — 1934 Crystal Springs in Forth Worth, Texas. http://thompsonian.info/brownies-calendar-1934.JPG.

Index

Note: Page numbers followed by "p" denotes photos

About the Author

Ralph G. Giordano holds a license as a professional Registered Architect in the State of New York, a Master's degree in Liberal Studies from the City University of New York, and a Bachelor's degree in Architecture from the New York Institute of Technology. He has authored four books:

- *Satan in the Dance Hall: The Rev. John Roach Straton, Social Dancing, and Morality in 1920s New York City* (Scarecrow 2008).
- *Social Dancing in America: Lindy Hop to Hip Hop 1901 to 2000 Volume Two* (Greenwood 2007).
- *Social Dancing in America: Fair Terpsichore to the Ghost Dance 1607 to 1900 Volume One* (Greenwood 2006).
- *Fun and Games in Twentieth-Century America: A Historical Guide to Leisure* (Greenwood 2003).

He is also serving as series editor for *The American Dance Floor* set. Giordano is a full-time teacher, architect, and an adjunct college Professor of History and American Studies.